THIRD GRADE TECHNOLOGY

32 LESSONS EVERY THIRD GRADER
CAN ACCOMPLISH ON A COMPUTER

FOURTH EDITION

Part Four of the Technology Curriculum by

Structured Learning

Fourth Edition 2011
Part Four of Structured Learning's Technology Curriculum
Visit the companion website at http://askatechteacher.com for more resources to teach technology to children

To receive a free weekly digital technology tip and/or website, send an email to admin@structuredlearning.net with the message "Subscribe to Weekly Tips" or "Subscribe to Weekly Websites"

ISBN 0-9787800-3-5

Printed in the United States of America

Introduction

This Structured Learning Technology Curriculum is designed to guide you and your child through a progressive growth of age-appropriate activities, resulting in a thorough knowledge of technology appropriate to your child's age level. If you didn't start with Kindergarten, go back and start there—even if your child is in third grade. There are skills taught there that aren't covered here, because it is assumed your child already learned them.

This Third Grade Textbook is aligned with National Educational Technology Standards for Students (see Appendix) to insure your child receives the broadest educational training available. It is based on a time-proven method successfully used and honed in classrooms. It requires a commitment of forty-five minutes a week of uninterrupted concentration on computers, followed up with two sessions of fifteen minutes each spread out throughout the week to practice keyboarding. If you can give more—that's great! If your time doesn't allow that as so many busy families don't, your child will still accomplish every goal within this book. The only rejoinder is: If there is a skill that

> "The problem with computers is they do what you tell them." — *Unknown.*

your child doesn't get, spend some additional time reinforcing and reminding. S/he won't get every skill the first time, but when you see it come up a second or third time through the course of these workbooks, then it's time to concentrate. Some skills are more difficult than others for some students. It doesn't mean your child can't accomplish it. It just means they need a bit of extra work.

The purpose of this textbook is not to teach the step-by-step details of the myriad computer skills. There are many fine books that will explain how to add Word borders, put a text box in Publisher, shade the cells in Excel and create a blog. What those books don't tell you is when your child is old enough to comprehend the skills they are teaching. That is what we do here: Guide you toward providing the right information at the right time, which allows your child the best opportunity to succeed. Just as most children can't learn to read at two, or write at four, they shouldn't be introduced to the fine motor skills of speed typing in kindergarten. We make sure your child gets what s/he needs, at the right age. The end result is a phenomenal amount of learning in a short period of time.

If there are skills that you don't know how to show your child that aren't 'taught' in this book, and you can't find books that address those in the manner you seek, you can visit the blog (AskATechTeacher.wordpress.com), the wiki and the internet start page that accompany this book (see publisher's website for more information). You'll find lots of help there.

Programs Required for K-5

Take a look at the list of programs we use. Some are free downloads (click links) or have free alternatives. The focus is programs that can collaborate with school projects, will teach critical skills, and can be used throughout the student's educational career. Here are the minimum requirements. Free alternatives are noted with links. If you don't have a pdf of this book, contact the publisher for a discounted copy:

General	(K-2)	Intermediate (3-5)
Outlook (or free Gmail)	KidPix (or free TuxPaint)	MS Office (or free Open Office, Google Docs)
Google Earth (free dl)	Type to Learn Jr. or	MS Publisher
Internet browser	free online keyboarding	Adobe Photoshop (or free Gimp)
	MS Office	Type to Learn (or free online keyboarding)
	MS Publisher	Oregon Trail (free online as classic edition)

Here's an overview of topics covered, as well as which grade. It tells you the topic, but not the skills—that comes later in this introduction. Some are covered every year, which means they are critical skills that don't go away and change with time. Some are learned early. These, once mastered, are not revisited, like mouse skills. After the addition of the second button and the scroll, not much changes with mouse skills.

	Mouse Skills	Vocabulary And Hardware	Problem-solving	Windows and the Basics	Keyboard and shortcuts	Adobe Photoshop	Word	PowerPoint	Publisher	Excel	Google Earth	E-Mail	Graphics
K	☺	☺	☺	☺	☺								☺
1	☺	☺	☺	☺	☺				☺		☺		☺
2		☺	☺	☺	☺		☺	☺	☺		☺		☺
3		☺	☺	☺	☺		☺	☺	☺	☺	☺	☺	
4		☺	☺		☺	☺	☺	☺	☺	☺	☺	☺	☺
5		☺	☺		☺	☺	☺		☺	☺	☺	☺	☺

Technology in general, and this curriculum specifically, builds on itself. What you learn a prior year will be used as you progress through the next grade level. For example, your child may have difficulty accomplishing the lessons laid out for fourth graders—say, typing 25 wpm with speed and accuracy—without going through those designated for grades K-3 sequentially. Have no fear, though: By the end of fifth grade, after following this series of lessons, they will accomplish everything necessary for Middle School.

Typical 45-minute Lesson

As you face a room full of eager faces, remember that you are a guide, not an autocrat. Use the Socratic Method—don't take over the student's mouse and click for them or type in a web address when they need to learn that skill. Even if it takes longer, guide them to the answer so they aren't afraid of how they got there. If you've been doing this since kindergarten, you know it works. In fact, by the end of kindergarten, you saw remarkable results.

When talking with students, always use the correct vocabulary. That's why I've included it on the lesson plan. Be sure to emphasize the vocabulary and expect students to understand it. Try the Vocabulary Board during one of the quarters/trimesters. Students love it and it highlights why they want to understand 'Geek Speak'.

Here's how I run a class:
- Students enter the room. They know to check the 'To Do' list on the overhead screen or Smart Board as they take their seats and plug their flash drive in. You're finishing up an email, but it doesn't matter. The beginning of class is student-directed.
- Students start with 10 minutes of typing practice, either using installed software or an online keyboarding program. Some days, they are directed to work on their site words in www.spellingcity.com or another active learning process that is self-directed.
- Next, there are three presentations (from *Google Earth Board*, *Problem-solving Board*, or *Vocabulary Board*). These rotate throughout the year, one per trimester/quarter. Students have selected their topic and presentation date. Whoever is up for the day will teach the class and take questions from the audience. This takes ten-twelve minutes. This week it's exploring the world with Google Earth.

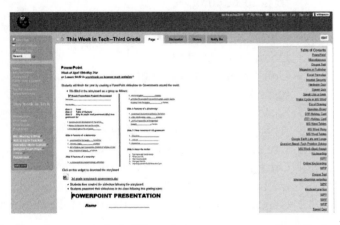

- If it's the beginning of a month, I review assigned homework and take questions. If it's the end of a trimester, I review which skills have been accomplished during the last three months.
- If we are starting a new project in our year of project-based learning, I review it with them, take questions and we start. If they are in the middle of one, they use the balance of the class to work towards its completion. I monitor activities, answer questions, help where needed. They have access to installed software and the internet which makes this portion of class student-centered learning requiring critical thinking and problem-solving skills

- During their work, students are free to post vocabulary words they don't understand on the vocabulary board and problem-solving ideas on that board.
- Students who have completed the current project take advantage of 'sponge activities' from a topic of their choice, practice keyboarding for the upcoming speed quiz or help a classmate struggling with a prickly skill. I include a variety of topical websites on a <u>class internet start page</u> (see inset for sample). Students know any websites on this page can be used by them during sponge time.
- Students who finish early may also access the <u>class wiki</u> (see inset for sample) to see what they might have missed in earlier classes.

How to Achieve Your Goals on a Weekly Basis

Here's how to be sure your child gets the most out of the time s/he spends on their technology education:

- ☐ Set aside 45 minutes for the core lesson and 15 minutes twice more during the week to reinforce.
- ☐ Sit straight with body centered in front of keyboard, legs in front of body, elbows at his/her sides.
- ☐ Place both hands in home-row position even though they use only one hand at a time. Let the other rest in home position waiting for its turn.
- ☐ Set book to left of keyboard—never in front of monitor.
- ☐ Remember: Parent/teacher is the guide—not the doer!
- ☐ Don't be distracted.
- ☐ Don't blame the computer. Always take responsibility.
- ☐ Save early. Save often.
- ☐ Always make a back-up of work.
- ☐ Use tech vocabulary during lesson.
- ☐ Once a problem solution is introduced (i.e., *what's today's date*), have the student do it the next time—don't do it for them!
- ☐ Check off each lesson item as the student accomplishes it.

> 1. When computing, whatever happens, behave as though you meant it to happen.
> 2. He who laughs last probably made a back-up.
> 3. If at first you don't succeed, blame your computer.
> 4. A complex system that does not work is invariably found to have evolved from a simpler system that worked just fine.
> 5. A computer program will always do what you tell it to do, but rarely what you want to do.
>
> *— Murphy's Laws of Computing*

TABLE OF CONTENTS

K-5 TECHNOLOGY SCOPE AND SEQUENCE

Check each skill off with I/W/M/C under '5' as student accomplishes it
(Column 1 refers to the ISTE Standard addressed by the skill)

ISTE		I=Introduced W=Working on M=Mastered C=Connected to Classwork	K	1	2	3	4	5
I		**Care and Use of the Computer**						
		Learn and practice safety on the Internet	I	W	W	W	M	C
		Keep your body to yourself—don't touch neighbor's kb	I	W	W	W	M	C
		Internet security—what it means, why	I	I	I	W	M	C
		Use of network file folders to save personal work	I	I	W	W	M	C
II		**Computer Hardware**						
		Understand how parts of the computer connect	I	W	M	C	C	C
		Know the names of all computer hardware	I	W	M	C	C	C
		Know how to adjust volume	I	W	M	C	C	C
		Know how to use the keyboard, mouse	I	W	M	C	C	C
		Know all parts of keyboard—Alt, F-row, space bar, etc	I	W	M	C	C	C
		Know how to turn monitor on/off	I	W	M	C	C	C
		Know how to power computer on, off	I	W	M	C	C	C
III		**Basic Computer Skills**						
		Know how to add file folders						I
		Know basic computer vocab—hardware and skills		I	W	M	C	C
		Understand Windows—desktop, icons, start button, etc.			I	W	M	C
		Understand the Ctr+Alt+Del, use of Task Manager				I	W	M
		Know how to drag-drop from one window to another						I
		Know how to log-on			I	W	M	C
		Know how to create a macro (for MLA heading)						I
		Understand mouse skills	I	W	M	C	C	C
		Understand right-click menus			I	W	M	C
		Know how to Open/Save/close a document, save-as, print	I	W	M	C	C	C
		Know how to solve common problems	I	W	M	C	C	C
		Know how to problem-solve with help files						I
		Understand tool bars in Word, Publisher, etc				I	W	M
		Know how to use flash drives—USB port, save-to, etc.				~~I~~	~~W~~	~~M~~
		Know how to use program you haven't been taught				I	W	M
		Know how to create wallpaper				I	W	M
		Understand differences/similarities between programs				I	W	M
IV		**Typing and Word Processing**						
	KB							
		Achieve age-appropriate speed and accuracy				I	W	M
		Know Alt, Ctrl, Backspace, spacebar, enter, tab, shift etc	I	W	M	C	C	C

		Know when to use cap key	I	W	M	C	C	C
		Know how to compose at keyboard		I	W	M	C	C
		Know correct spacing after words, sentences, paragraphs		I	W	M	C	C
		Use correct keyboarding posture	I	W	M	C	C	C
		Know how to use exclamation and question mark			I	W	M	C
		Understand F row				I	W	M
		Follow grammar/spelling rules	I	W	M	C	C	C
		Know when to use delete, backspace	I	W	M	C	C	C
		Know and use common keyboard shortcuts	I	W	M	C	C	C
		Know to put cursor in specific location, i.e., for graphic			I	W	M	C
		Be able to use online keyboarding sites			I	W	M	C
	WP							
		Understand Word basics			I	W	M	C
		Know how to move text within document					I	W
		Know how to use Ctrl+Enter to force a new page			I	W	M	C
		Know how to add a header/footer to a document			I	W	M	C
		Know how to format a document—fonts, borders, etc.			I	W	M	C
		Know how to use spell-check and grammar-check			I	W	M	C
		Know how to use word wrap				I	W	M
		Know how to insert pictures from clipart, file pic, internet			I	W	M	C
		Know how to insert tables				I	W	M
		Know how to insert text box						I
		Know how to create graphic organizers			I	W	M	C
		Know how to insert headers and footers			I	W	M	C
		Know how to create bullet lists and numbered lists					I	W
		Know how to outline						I
		Know print with print preview			I	W	M	C
		Know how to create and use an embedded link					I	W
		Understand Word pad, Notepad						I
V	**Designing (Photo, video, document)**							
		Introduce Digital cameras	I	I	I	I	I	I
		Know how to draw in one program and insert into another			I	W	M	C
		Insert geometric shapes into KidPix	I	W	W			
	Publisher							
		Know how to plan a publication			I	W	M	C
		Identify and understand parts of Publisher screen			I	W	M	C
		Know how to use tools, toolbars in Publisher			I	W	M	C
		Know how to add/edit text using the text box			I	W	M	C
		Know how to resize/move graphics			I	W	M	C
		Know how to use font schemes			I	W	M	C
		Know how to use color schemes			I	W	M	C

	Know how to add/delete a page, a picture or text				I	W	M
	Know how to insert a Table of Contents				I	W	M
	Know how to insert footer				I	W	M
	Know how to make a Card			I	W	M	C
	Know how to make a flier			I	W	M	C
	Know how to make a cover page				I	W	M
	Know how to make a simple storybook				I	W	M
	Know how to make a newsletter						I
	Know how to make a trifold brochure				I	W	M
	Know how to make a calendar						I

Photoshop

	Know how to plan a project						I
	Identify and understand the parts of the Photoshop screen						I
	Know how to use tools, toolbars in Photoshop						I
	Know how to add/edit text using the text box						I
	Know how to insert pictures (from clip art, file folder)						I
	Know how to use artistic renderings						I
	Know how to use auto fixes						I
	Know how to clone in a pic and across pictures						I
	Know how to crop with marquee, lasso tool, magic wand						I
	Know how to reset screen to default						I
	Know how to use history to go back in time						I
	Understand the use of 'layers' in constructing a project						I
	Know how to use the healing brush tool						I
	Know how to use filters						I
	Know how to replace backgrounds in pictures						I
	Know how to use 'Actions' tool on tool bar						I
	Know how to use art history brush						I
	Know how to use the paint brush						I

VI Presenting

	Introduce PowerPoint			I	W	M	C
	Understand layout, screen, tools, toolbars, placesavers			I	W	M	C
	Know how to insert text, edit, format			I	W	M	C
	Know how to insert pictures from file, internet, clip-art			I	W	M	C
	Understand how to add backgrounds to one or all slides			I	W	M	C
	Know how to insert animated GIF's/short movies			I	W	M	C
	Know how to insert animation into slides			I	W	M	C
	Know how to add transitions between slides			I	W	M	C
	Know how to add custom animations to slides			I	W	M	C
	Practice presentation skills			I	W	M	C
	Know how to have slides automatically			I	W	M	C
	Know how to insert interactive hyperlinks					I	W
	Know how to add/rearrange slides			I	W	M	C

	Know how to add music and sounds to one slide or many					I	W
	Understand and practice presentation skills			I	W	M	C
VII	**Spreadsheets**						
	Understand the layout, screen, tools, toolbars				I	W	M
	Know how to sort data				I	W	M
	Know how to format data				I	W	M
	Know how to use basic formulas				I	W	M
	Know how to recolor tabs and rename tabs				I	W	M
	Know how to widen columns and rows				I	W	M
	Know how to enter data and make a quick graph				I	W	M
	Know how to label x and y axis on graphs				I	W	M
	Know how to format a chart				I	W	M
	Know how to add a hyperlink to spreadsheet						I
	Know how to use print preview				I	W	M
	Know how to add headers/footers						I
VIII	**Internet basics**						
	Understand elements of an Internet address/URL			I	W	M	C
	Understand use of a start page	I	W	M	C	C	C
	Understand use of forward/back buttons, home, links		I	W	M	C	C
	Know how to use Bookmarks		I	W	M	C	C
	Understand difference between search and address bars	I	W	M	C	C	C
	Know how to use scroll bars	I	W	M	C	C	C
	Know how to save images and ethical considerations	I	W	M	C	C	C
	Know how to use the right click				I	W	M
	Know how to search and research on Google				I	W	M
	Know how to identify reliable sources on the internet				I	W	M
	Understand how to evaluate and identify reliable websites				I	W	M
	Web 2.0						
	Learn how to check grades online						I
	Understand Cloud computing (create a logo, avatar, etc.)				I	W	M
	Understand blogs and how to participate in them						1
	Understand an Internet start page and how to use it	I	W	M	C	C	C
	Understand internet Netiquette				I	W	M
	Understand class webpages, share info, upload files, etc.				I	W	M
IX	**Integrated — Multi-media**						
	Know how to follow directions in the use of computers	I	W	M	C	C	C
	Understand digital camera	I	W	M	C	C	C
	Know how to mix words and pictures to communicate	I	W	M	C	C	C
	Google Earth						

		Know how to find a location on Google Earth	I	W	M	C	C	C
		Know how to add a location to Google Earth's 'Places'				I	W	M
		Understand the use of latitudes and longitudes				I	W	M
		Know how to play a tour	I	W	M	C	C	C
		Know how to create a tour					I	W
		Know how to use Google Earth Community						I
		Know how to use the ruler to measure distances						I
	Email							
		Know how to email homework to teachers				I	W	M
		Understand parts of an email—subject, to, cc, message				I	W	M
		Understand and use proper email etiquette				I	W	M
		Understand the use of cc in an email				I	W	M
		Know how to attach a document to an email				I	W	M

Lesson #1—Introduction

Vocabulary	Problem solving	Collaborations
▣ *Digital* ▣ *multimedia* ▣ *Right mouse button* ▣ *Right-click menu* ▣ *Windows* ▣ *Back-up* ▣ *PC*	▣ *What if double-click doesn't work (push enter)* ▣ *What if monitor doesn't work (push power button)* ▣ *What if computer doesn't work (Is the mouse awake?)*	**"To go forward, you must backup."** *Cardinal rule of computing*
NETS-S: *6.a*		

Lesson questions? Go to http://askatechteacher.com

Review rules with students. Ask for suggestions from them for others you may not have mentioned

_____ No excuses; don't blame people; don't blame the computer

_____ Save early, save often—about every ten minutes is a good time-frame

_____ No food or drink around computer. Period.

_____ Respect the work of others and yourself

_____ Tour classroom. Show students where everything is, including the printer and the gallery of student work. Take this opportunity to review important posters on the wall, i.e., the difference between 'save' and 'save-as' and the difference between 'backspace' and 'delete'.

Review computer hardware. Remind students that the 'computer' is five parts:

_____ Mouse—left and right buttons, mouse wheel, click and double click

_____ CPU—point out the power button, CD drive, USB port

_____ Monitor—point out power button, screen

_____ Headphones—point out volume control and show them how to adjust the size

_____ Keyboard—home row, F4, enter, spacebar

_____ Power buttons—there are two: monitor and CPU

_____ Station number—behind monitor

Review homework policy

_____ Homework in back of this workbook, due via email

_____ Homework due monthly, last day of month

Take digital picture and AVI movie

_____ Discuss digital

_____ Discuss multimedia

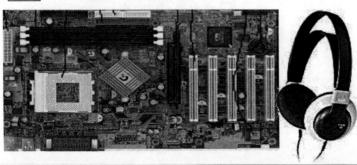

NAME THE PARTS OF THE COMPUTER

Name each part of the computer system on the line next to it.

WHAT'S THE DIFFERENCE BETWEEN SAVE AND SAVE AS?

SAVE

- Save the first time
- Resave changes to the same location

SAVE AS

- Resave under a new name
- Resave to a new location

Put this on the wall of your classroom/lab

TWO WAYS

TO DELETE

BACKSPACE

Deletes to the left, one character at a time

DELETE

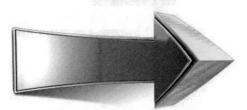

Deletes to the right, one character at a time

Lesson #2—Parts of the Computer

Vocabulary	Problem solving	Collaborations
☐ Escape ☐ Icon ☐ Desktop ☐ Tool bar ☐ Protocol ☐ User name	▪ *My mouse doesn't work (wake it up)* ▪ *My volume doesn't work (check volume control on systray)* ▪ *Where's the right mouse? (that's the right mouse button)* ▪ *How do I spell-check (right click or F7)*	▪ *Critical thinking* ▪ *Problem solving*
NETS-S: 6.a		

Lesson questions? Go to http://askatechteacher.com

Review parts of computer (see next pages)—quiz in two weeks

_____ Will include major parts (CPU, monitor, keyboard, mouse, headphones, USB port, peripherals, important keys). Quiz will look like study guide. Students are graded on spelling (because there's a word bank; all they have to do is copy).

Keyboard speed quiz today. Warm up with TTL4 (or online typing program—see appendix for suggested online sites).

_____ Give students 5-10 minutes to practice, then start speed quiz.

_____ Open MS Word. Review program layout—menu bar, ribbons, blinking cursor. Students will remember most of this from 2nd grade. Have students put heading at top of page (their name, teacher, date)

_____ Speed quiz is 5 minutes (see samples on next pages). Start/stop with buzzer. Tell students not to correct spelling/grammar mistakes during the test. You'll give them one minute to correct after buzzer. Remind them to use F7 or right click to correct spelling/grammar.

_____ At end of quiz, have students type their word count at bottom of quiz.

_____ Review grading policy with students—that their grade is based on their improvement (see next pages for breakdown). I give Free Dress Passes (we wear uniforms) to students who meet 15wpm. This is optional. I do find students who want that prize will practice and retake the quiz in an effort to win it (I allow them to retake all quizzes as often as they want without penalty).

_____ Save to file folder; Print for grading (suggest they use Ctrl+P)

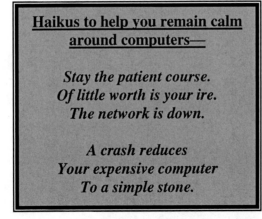

Haikus to help you remain calm around computers—

Stay the patient course.
Of little worth is your ire.
The network is down.

A crash reduces
Your expensive computer
To a simple stone.

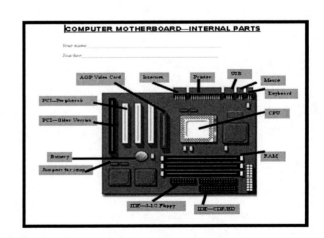

COMPUTER HARDWARE ASSESSMENT

_____ _Name_

_____ _Date_

Name each part of the computer hardware system on the line next to it

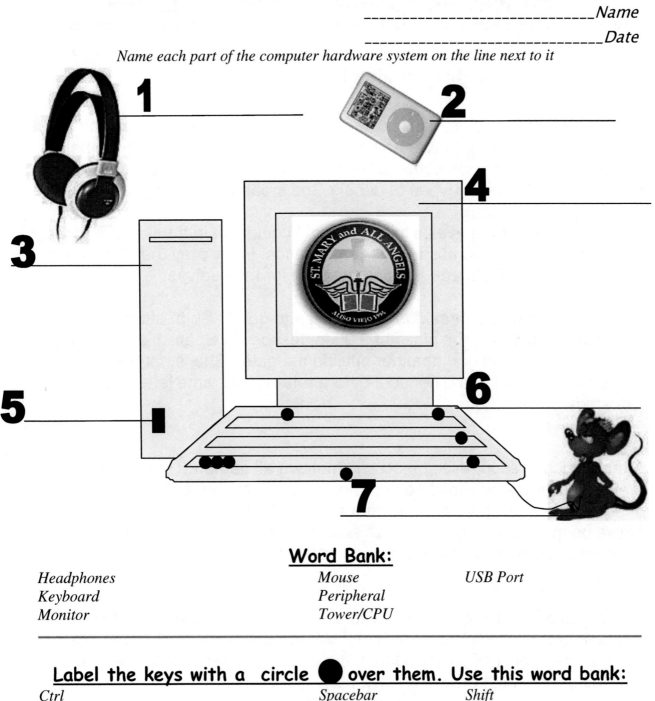

Word Bank:

Headphones	*Mouse*	*USB Port*
Keyboard	*Peripheral*	
Monitor	*Tower/CPU*	

Label the keys with a circle ⬤ **over them. Use this word bank:**

Ctrl	*Spacebar*	*Shift*
Alt	*Flying Windows*	*Enter*
Backspace	*F4*	

TWO KEYBOARDING SPEED QUIZZES

1. A day in the life of a Padre...

A.M.

I awoke before the dawn, as is customary for me and my fellow padre. I offered up my morning prayer and got dressed. At sunrise, I rang the bell and watched my mission come to life in the dawn. It is an amazing thing indeed to see the many types of people God created to live together.

At mass at 7:00 in the *iglesia* this morning, I could see in the faces of some of the Indians that God has touched their minds. I only pray that the others will follow in their footsteps and find the truth for themselves.

The bread and milk at breakfast was fresh and good. Soon after we ate, the children arrived in the plaza at 9:00 for lessons in Spanish and singing. Next I visited the old grandmother outside the gate. She is not well. I prayed for her health and her soul before returning to write letters to the Governor.

P.M.

After a lunch of soup, milk, bread and fruit, we all gathered in the *iglesia* to pray. After *siesta*, we finished our irrigation system. Our children stared open-mouthed as they saw the water rush by. I can see that many of the native people are proud of what we accomplish here. I hope this season will be a bountiful one and will provide enough food for our growing mission.

There was a birth today and the child will be baptized tomorrow. We will call him José Carlos in honor of San José and our beloved King Carlos. After a light supper of soup and fruit, the evening passed without event. I am weary, and must pray and sleep now. Farewell.

2. Tips on Good Study Habits

IN SCHOOL

Listen carefully. The instructor will often highlight key points. Take good notes. Learn how to outline. Write down only key points. Review them every day. Record your assignments. Get involved in class discussions. Think positively. Seek help from the instructor when necessary. Consider starting or belonging to a study group. Look at school as "your job." It is your primary responsibility. Do not miss school! Strive for perfect attendance. Always complete your assignments on time.

AT HOME

Set your study goals each day. Have a plan. Use your time wisely. Study in a place reserved just for study on a desk or a table. Clear your desk of all non-study material. If at all possible, study at the same time each day and study something every day. Become a better reader. Reading comprehension is the core of all good study and understanding. Take a course on how to read. Do not postpone term papers. Begin them as soon as they are assigned. Begin with an outline of what you want to say.

Use the Library for research and study. DO NOT PLAGIARIZE. Always give credit for what you write when it is someone else's idea. Use the internet carefully; check the quality of your resources. Read the newspaper, magazines, and articles, for background information or for just staying informed. Write all assignments on the computer. Back up your disks. Don't be afraid to get additional help from a tutor, aide, parent, fellow student whenever you can or need it.

Third-Fifth Grade Keyboarding Grading

By third grade, students are expected to use the good traits they've acquired in K-2 to improve keyboarding speed and accuracy. I give them a five-minute typing test once a trimester. They're graded on speed, accuracy, and typing habits. As they type, I walk around and anecdotally judge their posture, hand position, use of fingers, etc and deduct points if they are inadequate.

At the end of the five-minute quiz, I allow one minute to correct spelling errors.

Grading is based on improvement from their last quiz. A student who types 10 wpm could get a 7/10 if he didn't improve or a 10/10 if he improved from 8wom on the last quiz. Everyone gets 10/10 on the first quiz—a gift.

Here's the breakdown:

20% improvement:	*10/10*
10% improvement:	*9/10*
1-10% improvement:	*8/10*
No improvement:	*7/10*
Slowed down:	*6/10*

Since third graders are barely into percents, we discuss what that means.

I post a list of keyboard speedsters on the bulletin board. I also post the winning class (fastest) for all to see. Students who reach the grade level standard for speed and accuracy get a free dress pass (we are a uniform school). This is quite exciting for them.

Grade level standards are:

K-2	*None—work on good habits*
3rd Grade:	*15 wpm*
4th Grade:	*25 wpm*
5th Grade:	*30 wpm*

Lesson #3—Intro to Email

Vocabulary	Problem solving	Collaborations
☐ *Alt* ☐ *F4* ☐ *Etiquette* ☐ *Netiquette* ☐ *Attachments* ☐ *Email* ☐ *Flag* ☐ *Cc* ☐ *Bcc*	☐ *How do I close a program (Alt+F4)* ☐ *How do I move between cells (push tab key)* ☐ *How do I find lats and long (go to view-grid)*	☐ *Grammar* ☐ *Spelling* ☐ *Geography* ☐ *Organizing information*
NETS-S:		
3.a, 3.c		

Lesson questions? Go to http://askatechteacher.com

Practice Keyboarding using TTL4 or online sites. Remind students of proper posture.

_____ As they practice, share with them the biggest problems you observed as they took their speed quiz last week.

Review Homework Policy again—due last day of month at midnight, via email

_____ No late deductions this month, but there will be next month. It takes a while for 3rd graders and their parents to understand the use of email in school. Don't penalize this learning curve.

‖*Lesson Plan—Explain what email is and how to use it. Discuss email etiquette (see next pages). Review privacy considerations and best practices.*‖

_____ Open lab software for email. Review the layout. Remind students: There are many email programs. The one they have at home may be different from the school's. Ask parents to help students match what you teach with their system.

_____ Review fields in an email (To:, From:, cc:, bcc:, subject:) Use tab to move between fields. Remind students how important spelling address correctly is.

_____ Body of email: Be brief. Use correct grammar and spelling. You can include pictures, links, and text.

_____ Review how to attach a document and how to open one that is attached

_____ Review email etiquette (see list on next pages)

_____ Have students do a sample email. Walk around and be sure it's correct. Have them address it to you. This is a good opportunity to see if they know your email (for homework and projects). Experiment with the editing tools—they're similar to those in MS Word.

_____ Show students how to check the 'Sent' file to be sure their email went out. Show them how to ask for a receipt. Encourage them to do this with emails they send to you

_____ Go over the hints on the next page. Take them slowly. Encourage discussion on items like email security, spam, etc

Review Hardware for next week's quiz

_____ Have students complete the study guide under Lesson #2 and use as reference

EMAIL ETIQUETTE

1. Use proper formatting, spelling, grammar

2. CC anyone you mention

3. Subject line is a quick summary of what your email discusses

4. Use correct subject line protocol—lastname-grade-topic (lastname3hw2)

5. Answer received emails swiftly

6. Re-read your email before sending

7. Don't use capitals—THIS IS SHOUTING

8. Don't leave out the subject line

9. Don't attach unnecessary files

10. Don't overuse the high priority

11. Don't email confidential information

12. Don't email offensive remarks

13. Don't forward chain letters or spam

14. Don't open attachments from strangers

Lesson #4—Problem Solving

Vocabulary	Problem solving	Collaborations
☐ *back space* ☐ *escape* ☐ *capital* ☐ *caps lock* ☐ *monitor power* ☐ *CPU power* ☐ *monitor* ☐ *double click* ☐ *tools* ☐ *icons* ☐ *tool bar* ☐ *log on*	☐ *Volume doesn't work (check the control in the systray)* ☐ *Monitor doesn't work (check the power)* ☐ *Computer doesn't work (check the power)* ☐ *Capital doesn't work (Is caps lock on?)* ☐ *What is today's date (check clock in lower right corner)* ☐ *How do I exit a program (file-exit or Alt+F4)*	☐ *Problem-solving skills* ☐ *Creative-thinking skills*
NETS-S:		
6.a, 6.c		

Lesson questions? Go to http://askatechteacher.com

Hardware Quiz today (see previous lesson for quiz sample)

_____ Any questions before beginning

_____ Give ample time, but not too much to get frustrated

_____ If a student didn't do as well as they hoped, allow them to retake for full credit. Few will and those that do will work extra-hard to do better the next time.

Those who finish can practice keyboarding on TTL4 or an online site like DanceMat Typing until all students finish quiz

_____ When everyone's done, review keyboard shortcuts (shortkeys) with students (see next page). Go over the most common ones. Start using these. For example, instead of using File-exit to close a program, suggest students use Alt+F4. When saving, use Ctrl+S. Students love shortkeys. They will challenge each other to see who can get a task done fastest, most efficiently.

Review Problem solving—

_____ Do this like Q&A—ask the question; see who can answer the fastest. Use the problems above and those on the next pages.

_____ Make this fun and an intro to the upcoming Problem Solving Board

Sign up for Problem Solving Board—presentations start in two weeks (see next pages).

_____ Students can sign up before/after school, lunch, any time they're free.

_____ Review how you'll grade them (see next pages)

_____ Sign up for a date to present. They will tell their classmates their problem, how to solve it and take questions. It takes only about three minutes.

_____ Sign up for a problem. Students can get the solution from family, friends, neighbors or even the teacher as a last resort. They are responsible for teaching their classmates how to solve the problem.

Most popular shortkeys students will love using:

Maximize window	Double click title bar
Quick Exit	Alt+F4
Date and Time	Shift+Alt+D = Date
	Shift+Alt+T = Time
Show taskbar	WK (Windows key)
Shows desktop	WK+M

Ctrl Key Combinations

CTRL+C: Copy	CTRL+P: Print
CTRL+X: Cut	CTRL+K: Add hyperlink
CTRL+V: Paste	CTRL+E: Center align
CTRL+Z: Undo	CTRL+L: Left align
CTRL+B: Bold	CTRL+R: Right align
CTRL+U: Underline	CTRL+ : Zoom in Internet
CTRL+I: Italic	CTRL- : Zoom out Internet

Fun Keyboard Shortcuts:

<+=+> = ⇔

—+> = →

:+) = ☺

Add Your Favorite:

_____

_____

Most common problems students face while using computers:

	Problem	Solution
1	My browser is too small	Double click the blue bar
2.	Browser tool bar missing	Push F11
3.	Exit a program	Alt+F4
4.	Today's date	Hover over clock Shift+Alt+D in Word
5.	Double click doesn't work	Push enter
7.	Start button disappeared	Use Windows button
8.	Program disappeared	Check taskbar
9.	Erased my document	Ctrl+Z
10.	I can't find a tool	Right click on screen; it'll show most common tools
11.	My screen is frozen	Clear a dialogue box Press Escape four times
12.	My menu command is grey	Press escape 4 times and try again
13.	Can't find Bold, Italic, Underline	Use Ctrl+B, Ctrl+I, Ctrl+U

Put this on your walls:

UNDO

is your
Friend

Problem Solving Board Sign-up

	Teacher #1	Teacher #2	Teacher #3
Week of October 2nd			
Week of October 9th			
Week of October 16th			
Week of October 23rd			
Week of October 30th			
Week of November 6th			
Week of November 13th			
Week of November 27th			

	Teacher #1	Teacher #2	Teacher #3
What if the double-click doesn't work			
What if the monitor doesn't work			
What if the volume doesn't work			
What if the computer doesn't work			
What if the mouse doesn't work			
What's the right-mouse button for?			
What's the keyboard shortcut to close a program			
How do I move between cells or boxes?			
How do I figure out today's date?			
What if the capital doesn't work			
What if my toolbar disappears			
What if the document disappears			
Keyboard shortcut for 'undo'			
How do I search for a file			
What if the program disappears			
What if the program freezes			
What is the protocol for saving a file			
What is the protocol for the subject line in an email			
What does 'CC' mean in an email			
How do I get out of a screen I'm stuck in			
How do I double space in Word			
How do I add a footer in Word			
How do I add a watermark in Word			
How do I make a macro in Word			
How do I add a border in Word			
How do I add a hyperlink in Word			
Keyboard shortcuts for B, I, U			

PROBLEM SOLVING BOARD
GRADE

Name: _____

Class: _____

_____
_____

Knew question   _____

Knew answer   _____

Asked audience for help if you didn't know answer_____

No umm's, stutters   _____

No nervous movements (giggles, wiggles, etc.)   _____

Overall   _____

Lesson #5—Graphic Organizers I

Vocabulary	Problem solving	Collaborations
☐ *Font* ☐ *Alignment* ☐ *Tools* ☐ *Tool bar* ☐ *Menu bar* ☐ *Drop-down menus* ☐ *Formatting*	☐ *My tool bar disappeared* ☐ *I can't close down (try Alt+F4)* ☐ *Where's my diagram toolbar (select the diagram so handles show and you'll find it)*	☐ *Grammar* ☐ *Spelling* ☐ *Science*
<center>NETS-S: *2.b, 4.d*</center>		

Lesson questions? Go to http://askatechteacher.com

Start the day with keyboard practice—Type to Learn or an online typing site. Review good posture tenants (see next pages) with students.

_____ Take a few minutes to review the location of the most important keys on the keyboard (see next pages for what they are)

Lesson Plan—Use MS Word target diagram to organize the Universe. Start with the student's town in the center and build out. Show students how to color the diagram. For olders. This is a great way to show kids how they can organize their thoughts with pictures, diagrams, tables—lots of ways other than simple text.

_____ Open Word. Review menus, ribbons, page layout.

_____ Put heading (name-teacher-date) at top of page

_____ Add title 'WHERE WE ARE' and center

_____ Insert nested Venn diagram (insert-Smart Art); add shapes until you have six

_____ Fill each level in from county in center to the galaxy; watch grammar and spelling

_____ Format the graphic organizer as you like with the ribbon tools

_____ This will take most of the class, but that's fine. Be prepared to discuss each level with the class—What's the name of our solar system? Are there more than one Universes?

_____ Advanced: Add a table at the bottom to show another way to organize this same information.

Close down

_____ Save project to your file folder as "lastname 3 diagram"; save-as to flash drive (find 'removable disk'). Remind students of the difference between 'save' and 'save-as'.

If students finish early, go to class internet start page for Sponge websites.

> ## "A computer does what you tell it to do, not what you want it to do."

Assume the Position

- Legs centered in front of body
- Body centered in front of keyboard
- Hands curved over home row
- Document to left of computer
- Use right thumb for space bar
- Eyes on screen

KEYS YOU SHOULD KNOW

IMPORTANT KEYBOARD KEYS

WHERE WE ARE

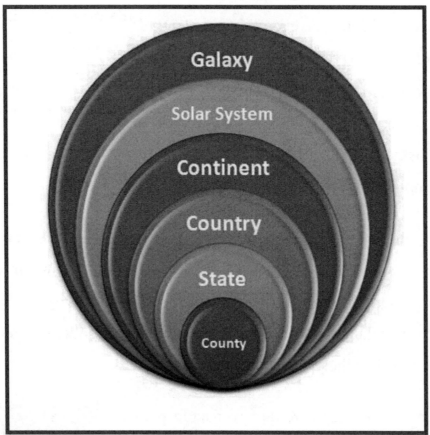

My city	
My county	
My state	
My country	USA
My continent	North America
My hemisphere	Northern Hemisphere
My planet	Earth
My solar system	The Solar System
My galaxy	The Milky Way

Using an Internet Start Page

An internet start page is the first page that comes up when students select the 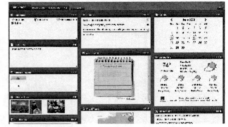 internet icon. It should include everything students visit on a daily basis (typing websites, research locations, sponge sites) as well as information specific to the current project, class guidelines, the day's 'to do' list, and a calculator. It is one of the great ways teachers can make internetting simpler and safer for their students.

Mine includes oft-used websites, blog sites, a To Do list, search tools, email, a calendar of events, pictures of interest, rss feeds of interest, weather, news, a graffiti wall and more. Yours will be different. I used protopage.com, but you can use netvibes or pageflakes.com. Each comes with its own collection of installable 'widgets' to personalize the page to your needs.

Start pages are an outreach of the ever-more-popular  social networking. Most search engines offer them also (try iGoogle at www.google.com/ig). They all have a huge library of custom fields (called 'flakes' on Pageflakes) to individualize any home page. And, they're all simple. Don't be intimidated.

When you get yours set up, on the To Do list, put what the child should do to start each computer time. This gives them a sense of independence, adultness, as they get started while you're wrapping something else up.

See open letter on next page about how I use more Web 2.0 tools to better communicate with parents and students.

A Note to My Readers : How I Use Web 2.0 Tools in My Classroom to Communicate with Parents

I've been teaching for over twenty years in different schools, different communities, but one factor transcends grades, classes, and culture: Parents want to be involved with what's going on at their children's school. Parent-teacher communication is vital and in my experience, the number one predictor of success for a student. But parents can't always get in to the classroom as a volunteer and see what's written on the white board. They can't always make the school meetings to hear the comings and goings of the school. Why? It's not lack of interest. More likely, they're working; doing that 8-5 thing that insures the future of their families and pays for their children's college education.

Knowing the importance of parent involvement, I feel that my job as a teacher includes not just the lessons I share with students but keeping my parents informed on classroom happenings. I need to be as transparent as possible, get as much information as I can out to parents in a manner they can understand and a format they can access. If I could tape my classes and post them on YouTube, or offer a live feed during class, I would. But I can't, so I try other creative ideas.

Class website
This is teacher directed, but gives me a chance to communicate class activities, pictures, homework, and extra credit opportunities–all the little details that make up a class–with parents. This is a first stop to understanding what's going on in class.

Class wiki
This is student-directed, student-centered. Students post summaries of their tech class, examples of their work, projects they've completed on the wiki for everyone to share. This way, parents see the class through the eyes of the students. And so do I, which is my way of assuring that what I think happened, did.

Twitter
I love tweets because they're quick, 140 character summaries of activities, announcements, events. They take no time to read and are current.

Emails
I send lots of these out with reminders, updates, FAQs, discussion of issues that are confusing to parents. I often ask if I'm sending too many, but my parents insist they love them.

Open door
I'm available every day after school, without an appointment. Because I have so many other ways to stay in touch, my classroom rarely gets so crowded that I can't deal with everyone on a personal level.

Lesson #6—Graphic Organizers II

Vocabulary	Problem solving	Collaborations
☐ *F keys* ☐ *Diagram* ☐ *SmartArt* ☐ *3-D* ☐ *Autoformat* ☐ *Home row* ☐ *automaticity*	☐ *What if log-on doesn't work? (Did you spell user name and password correctly?)* ☐ *How do I close a program (Alt+F4)* ☐ *Select-do (always select before doing)* *What if a menu command is grayed-out? (push escape four times)*	☐ *Grammar* ☐ *Spelling* ☐ *Science*
NETS-S: *2.b; 4.b*		

Lesson questions? Go to http://askatechteacher.com

Keyboarding—Type to Learn (TTL4) or online typing site—log on with class, your name
Problem-solving board presentations start today (and every week).

_____ See grading rubric under Lesson #4.

"Where in the World" project—Week 2 of 2

_____ Finish labeling each layer of organizer—remember grammar/spelling

_____ Select 'Design' from the menu bar (be sure to select diagram first)

_____ Pick 'change colors' and pick a color scheme—try different ones

_____ Double check the project for detail—heading on top left; title centered; diagram below title and centered.

Close down

_____ Save project to your file folder; save-as to flash drive; File name "lastname 3 diagram". Prompt students to understand why they save once and save-as once.

_____ Print; close Word (file-close or Alt+F4)

Those who finish, go to sponge sites on a topic recommended by the teacher (or see list on next pages). Math automaticity is always popular, or science/history. Check appendix for list by subject.

Comic credit: Isaacman

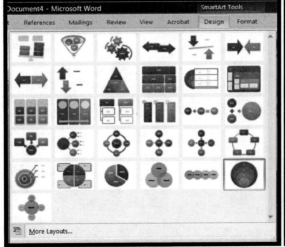

If you have time for an MS Word assessment, here's one. I sometimes squeeze it in when the students are ahead on a project. Use the graph on the next page to evaluate their skills so you know what they remember and what they don't:

WORD ASSESSMENT

Follow the instructions below. Part of the assessment is how well you read and complete directions. Do your best. If you don't remember how to do a skill, go on to the next.

- Put your heading on page
- Right-align heading
- Put a title underneath heading——"Word Assessment"
- Center the title, font Comic Sans, font size 14, bold
    - Type two paragraphs about your summer, font size 12, Times New Roman
- Change the second paragraph to font size 16 and Papyrus
- Add bullets with
    1. Your daily activities
    2. What you ate
    3. Who you played with
- Add "The End" as WordArt at the bottom of the page
- Add a border

Wherever you are, be there until you leave.
—mom

- Add a picture
- Have text wrap around the clipart
- Put a call-out aimed at the picture
- Add an autoshape
- Color the autoshape pink or red
- Insert a footer
    - Add a text box with what your mom

said the most this summer
- Shade the text box
- Add a table with seven columns and three times during the day
- Add information for each day and each time of day

This is easy!!!

Sunday	Monday	Tuesday	Wednesday	Thursday	Friday	Saturday
Ate breakfast						
Ate lunch						
Ate dinner						

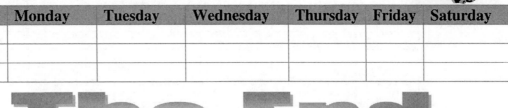

WORD ASSESSMENT

Question		1	2	3	4	5	6	7	8	9	10	11	12	13	14	15	16	17	18	19	20
																		STUDENT			
1	heading																				
	all parts																				
2	right align																				
3	title																				
	underneath																				
4	center																				
	Comic sans																				
	size 14																				
	Bold																				
5	2 paragraphs																				
	size 12																				
	TNR																				
6	Para. 2																				
	size 16																				
	Papyrus																				
7	bullets																				
	daily activities																				
	ate																				
	played w/																				
8	The End																				
	Wordart																				
	page bottom																				
9	border																				
10	picture																				
11	text wrap																				
12	call-out																				
	location																				
13	autoshape																				
14	pink																				
15	footer																				
16	text box																				
	mom's words																				
17	shade text box																				
18	table																				
	7 columns																				
	3 rows																				
	heading row																				
19	table into																				
Total		0	0	0	0	0	0	0	0	0	0	0	0	0	0	0	0	0	0	0	0

Thirty-two Ways to Use Spare Classroom Time

I keep a list of themed websites that are easy-in easy-out for students. They must be activities that can be accomplished enjoyably in less than ten minutes. In the parlance, these are called "sponges".

You may have read my post with <u>nineteen sites my students love visiting</u> during sponge time (let me know if you liked them, have some to add, I'm always interested in learning from you). Here are thirty-two more. Hope you like them!

Language Arts

- <u>Make your own Story</u>—answer questions, and the story writes itself
- <u>Funny poetry</u> to read and enjoy
- <u>Jeff's Poetry for Kids</u>
- <u>Fill in the blank poetry</u>
- <u>Get Writing</u>—write your own story
- <u>Web version of Mad Libs</u>

Math

- <u>Math and Virtual Manipulatives</u>
- <u>Math website</u>—popular, a standard
- <u>Math—by Grade Level</u>
- <u>Math—game-oriented</u>
- <u>Mental Math</u>
- <u>Minute Math</u>

Research

- <u>All-around research site</u>
- <u>Research for kids</u>
- <u>School Tube</u>—learning videos organized by topics
- <u>World Book Online</u>
- <u>Research—chapters on subjects</u>
- <u>National Geographic for kids</u>
- <u>Nova video programs</u>

Science

- <u>Videos on science topics</u>
- <u>Visit a Virtual Farm</u>
- <u>Virtual weather, machines and surgery</u>
- <u>National Geographic Kids</u>
- <u>NOVA Videos</u>—great topics Nova video programs
- <u>Science Headlines</u>—audio (grades 3+)
- <u>Great site on yucky stuff</u>
- <u>Virtual tours</u>

Technology

- <u>Virtual tours</u>
- <u>Webcams around the World</u>
- <u>More Worldwide webcams for kids</u>
- <u>Nova video programs</u>
- <u>School Tube</u>—learning videos from YouTube. Organized by topics

Lesson #7—Rebus Project in Word I

Vocabulary	Problem solving	Collaborations
☐ Rebus ☐ Ctrl ☐ Menu bar ☐ Ribbon ☐ Spell-check ☐ Right-click ☐ Synonyms	☐ What if program disappears (look on taskbar)? ☐ What is today's date?(Shift+Alt+D) ☐ I can't find my document/my file folder (go to Start-Search) ☐ Select-do (Always select what you want to work on before doing)	☐ Grammar ☐ Spelling ☐ Composition
	NETS-S: _1.b; 2.b_	

Lesson questions? Go to http://askatechteacher.com

Type to Learn—goal is 15 wpm by the end of 3rd grade

_____ Correct posture, legs in front; hands in home row, curved over keys

_____ Show students how to track where they are in the software's lessons

Remember: Homework due the end of each month

MS Word Rebus project—Week 1 of 2—preparation

_____ Open MS Word; use icon on desktop or Start button

_____ Start with your heading—name, teacher, date

_____ Use keyboard shortcut for date (Shift+Alt+D)

_____ Copy the story on next page including crossed out words and misspellings—don't change them!

_____ Use right-click to correct misspellings – this is spell check

_____ Use right-click to find synonyms for crossed out words. Explain what a 'synonym' is. Explain why we use synonyms and how they tweak the meaning of a sentence. Go over a few with them—synonyms for 'run', 'looked'. Do them as a group before students start this part of the project.

_____ Have students do as many of the items in the text box (see next page) as possible without assistance. These skills were done in second grade so this is review. Give students only 10-15 minutes to do this. Let them know it isn't graded and we'll go over them together.

_____ Print and turn in (Ctrl+P)

_____ Now have students write their own story that starts "Once upon a spooky Halloween…" Students will have the rest of the class to do this.

_____ Save to network(Ctrl+S); save-as to flash drive (what's the difference?)

Close down to desktop (Click all red 'xs' and save, or Alt+F4)

"Error, no keyboard – press F1 to continue."

Rebus Title

One very ~~spoowky~~ Halloween a ~~little~~ boy and his <u>frends</u> went out for a ~~fun~~ night of trick-or-treating. Little did they know, it would be a ~~night~~ they would not soon forget!!!

HALLOWEEN STORY

Name_____

Date_____

Teacher_____

Halloween

One very spoowky Halloween a ~~little~~ boy and his frends went out for a ~~fun~~ night of trick-or-treating. Little did they know, it would be a ~~night~~ they would not soon ferget!!!

Correct all misspellings. Find synonyms for crossed out words

> ### Add
> * = extra
> 1. Title in WA
> 2. Border
> 3. Spell-check
> 4. Grammar check
> 5. Thesaurus
> 6. Finish story
> 7. 3 fonts
> 8. 3 colors
> 9. 3 graphics
> 10. 3 sizes of fonts
> 11. *Footer**
> 12. *Watermark**

Lesson #8——Rebus Project in Word II

Vocabulary	Problem solving	Collaborations
☐ Clip-art ☐ Font ☐ Cursor ☐ Blinking ☐ 'X' ☐ Watermark	☐ What if double-click doesn't work? (push enter) ☐ What if program disappears (look on taskbar)? ☐ My picture looks weird (only use corners to resize)	☐ Spelling ☐ Grammar ☐ Composition ☐ Evaluating ideas
NETS-S: _1.b, 2.b_		

Lesson questions? Go to http://askatechteacher.com

Type to Learn or online typing website—goal is 15 wpm by the end of third grade

_____ Correct posture, legs in front; hands in home row, curved over keys

Lesson Plan—Students write a brief story in MS Word then add fonts, font sizes, font colors, a border, pictures—all skills learned last year. Those who can should add the more advanced skills of a watermark and word wraps

_____ Find Word; double click to open; open story saved last week

_____ Spell check (right-click on red squiggly lines); grammar-check (right-click on green squiggly lines); right-click on common words and go to 'synonyms'. Now that the story is written, add the title in WordArt (another 2nd grade skill).

_____ Change font/size/color for 3 words by clicking inside a word (not highlighting)

_____ Add a border. Be sure it's a 'page border'. Make it festive

_____ Click with mouse where you want a picture. Notice blinking cursor. That's where the image will go. Search for 3 images of 3 words and insert

_____ Use handles to resize image larger or smaller. Story must fit on one page.

_____ Check Print Preview to be sure story on one page. Save to file folder and save-as to flash drive. Discuss the difference between 'save' and 'save-as'.

_____ Print (Ctrl+P)

Close down to desktop (Click all 'x's and save, or Alt+F4)

Dr. Seuss for the techie child:
_You can think up web pages.
That's what you can do.
You can think them in yellow
With letters bright blue...
Think your banners in red.
And your buttons in pink.
You can paste in a JPEG.
Oh, the LINKS you can Link!
Credit: Gene Ziegler_

Halloween Story

One **spooky** Halloween a little boy and his **friends** went out for a **fun** night of **trick-o-treating**.

Little did they know it would be a night **THEY** would not soon forget!!! It was a **very scary night**.

*Name*_____

*Teacher's Name*_____

HALLOWEEN REBUS
GRADING RUBRIC—3rd GRADE

1. Heading with name, date, teacher   _____
2. A WordArt title, centered   _____
3. Several lines of story   _____
   - a. 3 different fonts   _____
   - b. 3 different size fonts   _____
   - c. 3 different colors   _____
   - d. Spell-check   _____
   - e. Grammar-check   _____
4. 3 inline pictures—all the same size   _____
5. A festive border   _____
6. *Watermark**   _____
7. *Footer**   _____
8. Story fills one page but not more   _____
   - a. Check Print Preview   _____
9. Professional appearance   _____

*=Extra credit

Q: What story do baby ghosts love to hear at bed time?

A: Ghoul Deluxe and the Three Scares
http://www.kidsdomain.com/holiday/halloween/games/jokes.html

Lesson #9—Tables in Word I

Vocabulary	Problem solving	Collaborations
☐ Table	☐ My document disappeared (Ctrl+Z to undo)	☐ Science
☐ Formatting		☐ Grammar
☐ Tab key	☐ My monitor doesn't work (push power button, check cables)	☐ Spelling
☐ Columns		☐ Vocabulary
☐ Rows	☐ Start button disappeared (press flying windows)	
☐ Cells		

NETS-S:
3.a; 3.b; 6.a

Lesson questions? Go to http://askatechteacher.com

Keyboard—Use TTL4 or online site. Remember that speed and accuracy count

_____ Hands curved over home row; body square in front of keyboard

_____ Good posture and hand position; elbows at sides; eyes on screen

Lesson Plan— In this tie-in to classroom inquiry into landforms, students design a 3 column table in Word to explore the types and examples of landforms. Collect data as a group so the class has an opportunity to share their knowledge.

_____ Open Word and put standard heading at top of page—name, teacher, date. Use keyboard shortcut for date (Shift+Alt+D)

_____ Make table with 3 columns, 5 rows—we'll add extra rows as needed

_____ Add heading to each column—'landform', 'example', picture'

_____ Tab to move on to next row and type the first landform. Discuss the definition of this. Tab to next column (Examples). Discuss examples of the landform—add one in the USA and one somewhere else in the world.

_____ Tab-tab to cell under first landform and type next one. Tab to next column. Discuss examples of this landform. Again, add one national, one international.

_____ Continue with the other landforms.

_____ When in last cell, pushing tab will add another row

_____ Give them time to explore landforms. They'll add pictures next week.

Close down to desk top with 'x' or Alt+F4

_____ Save to your file folder and save-as to flash drive. Ask students what the difference is.

LANDFORM	EXAMPLES	PICTURES
Mountain	Mt. Everest	
River	Mississippi River	
Ocean	Pacific Ocean	
Desert	Sahara Desert	
Forest	Amazon Rainforest	
Plains	Midwest African Savanna	

"Now, if you can find the power switch, flip it on."

LANDFORMS

Landform	Example	Picture
Forest	Amazon Rain Forest Red Wood forest	
Ocean	Pacific Ocean Indian Ocean	
Desert	Sahara Desert Gobi Desert	
Rivers	Nile River Mississippi River	
Lake	Lake Michigan Lake Victoria	
Mountain	Mount Fuji Mount McKinley	
Plain	Savannah Plain Great Plains	
Valley	Death Valley Nile Valley	
Glaciers	Antarctica Glaciers Alaska Glaciers	

Lesson #10—Tables in Word II

Vocabulary	Problem solving	Collaborations
☐ Tool ☐ Cell ☐ Row ☐ Column ☐ Right-click ☐ Greeting	☐ My capitals are stuck on (Is your caps lock on?) ☐ How do I log on (enter user name and password) ☐ What's today's date? (Shift+Alt+D) ☐ How do I add a row (tab from last cell)	☐ Grammar ☐ Spelling ☐ Science ☐ Humanities

<u>NETS-S:</u>
3.a; 3.b; 6.a

Lesson questions? Go to http://askatechteacher.com

Keyboard—good posture, body in front of keyboard, eyes on screen

_____ Type to Learn or online site—log on and continue through lessons; concentrate on speed and accuracy

Take time to review tips on next page. There are a few students have not yet seen.

Open MS Word—Landform project—week 2 of 2

_____ Finish any landforms and examples (column 1 and 2) not completed

_____ Go to Google Images; search for pictures of landforms. Give students time to be amazed by the wonders of our planet. You will hear lots of exclamations as they are stunned by Earth's beauty.

_____ Select an example. Right-click and copy; select MS Word on taskbar; right-click and paste into cell; resize. Repeat for each landform picture

_____ Alternative: Go to Google Earth; find landform on globe; save picture and insert into column

_____ Advanced: add a fourth column with a fact. Allow students to chat with neighbors to come up with this data.

_____ Advanced: shade row for column headings (see example on previous page)

_____ Save (Ctrl+S); save-as to flash drive; print (Ctrl+P)

For those who are done, make a Thanksgiving card in Publisher using 2nd grade skills.

_____ Add greeting, their name, pictures, to whom it goes

Close down to desk top with 'x' or Alt+F4

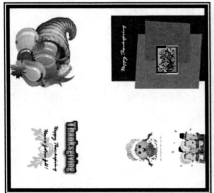

Chaos reigns within.
Reflect, repent, and reboot.
Order shall return.

- - - - - - - - -

Program aborting:
Close all that you have worked on.
You ask far too much.

Your file was so big.
It might be very useful.
But now it is gone.

- - - - - - - - -

The Web site you seek
Cannot be located, but
Countless more exist.

6 MS Word Tricks Every Student Should Know

The faster you teach students to be problem solvers, the more they'll learn. Computers are a foreign language. Even with small class sizes, the more students can do for themselves, the more fun they'll have learning the intricacies of technology.

The good news is, students love to be independent. They find it cool to know keyboard shortcuts for getting stuff done. In my class, students can help their neighbors, and they love showing off their problem solving skills. Here are 9 tricks that cover many common problems students will face using MS Word:

1. Ctrl+Z—undo
This will be their favorite. There are too many times to mention when I've had a frantic student, almost in tears because s/he thought s/he'd lost his/her document, and two seconds later, I retrieved it. I was the hero for a class period.

2. How to find lost documents
It takes a while for users to get accustomed to saving files on a network. Often, documents end up lost (in my school, students must drill down through five levels to get to their unique location). My students learn early to use **'search' on the start menu**.

3. How to insert data
The 'insert' key is so confusing I'm told it is being de-activated in the future. If students complain they lose data as they type, this is probably why. Show them how to **push the 'insert' key** and all will be fixed.

4. Show-hide tool.
Kids try to strong-arm Word into doing their will—often the wrong way. My favorite is 'enter enter' as a shortcut to double space. It seems to work until they have to edit the document, and then everything gets messed up. Have students push the **show-hide button** to see if they're using the double space tool. Then, show them where the icon is.

5. Tables—they work so much better than columns and tabs.
Teach it to kids **early and use it often**. It will save miles of distress.

6. How to insert the date
It takes until Middle School for students to remember the date. Before that, they will always ask. Show them the **Shift+Alt+D** shortkey that inserts the current date into Word. They love it and it saves a lot of time for you.

Lesson #11—Thanksgiving Greetings

Vocabulary	Problem solving	Collaborations
☐ *Greeting* ☐ *Border* ☐ *Page border* ☐ *Format* ☐ *Watermark*	☐ *I can't find a tool (right click on page for commonly used tools)* ☐ *The font is too big on the flier (Publisher readjusts size as needed; keep typing)*	☐ *Spelling* ☐ *Grammar* ☐ *Creative writing*
NETS-S: *1.b; 2.b*		

Lesson questions? Go to http://askatechteacher.com

Sign up for Speak Like a Geek Vocabulary presentations (see next pages)

_____ Students define word, use it in a sentence, take questions. It takes about three minutes. One way to find def: Go to Google; type *define:yourword* in search bar. Google provides definitions. Pick one that fits tech.

_____ Or, students can get def from family, friends, or teacher as last resort.

_____ Presentations start after the holidays

Lesson Plan— Students write a brief Thank You to parents using skills already learned in MS Word. Reinforce concepts of grammar and spelling being covered in their classroom.

_____ Give students ample time to type their poem or note to parents thanking them for whatever is on their minds.

_____ When done, students select entire piece, change font size to 14-18 (depending upon how much they wrote). Then select a font. Try different ones until they find one they like.

_____ Add a title in Word Art. Then add an art border

_____ Add Thanksgiving pictures; picture will go where your cursor is blinking

_____ Advanced: Add a watermark that says 'Happy Thanksgiving'

_____ Done? Create Thanksgiving flier in Publisher (see below) using 2nd grade skills

_____ Save (Ctrl+S), save as to flash drive, print (Ctrl+P). Ask students what is the difference between 'save' and 'save-as'?

Close down to desk top with 'x' or Alt+F4

Alternative to Thanksgiving letter: A Rebus

Have students write a story and add at least five pictures inline that communicate the words.

Marcy and Mathew were both looking forward to Thanksgiving dinner. They knew they would have baked and a **great BIG** of mashed and sauce and on the cob. They knew they would have a of cranberry sauce and for dessert. BUT, and wanted to have a like all their friends had for Thanksgiving.

Speak Like a Geek

	Teacher #1	Teacher #2	Teacher #3
Week of Jan 24th			
Week of Jan. 31st			
Week of March 7th			
Week of March 14th			
Week of March 28th			
Week of April 11th			
Week of April 18th			
Week of April 25th			
Week of May 2nd			

	Teacher #1	Teacher #2	Teacher #3
.com			
.gif, .bmp, .jpg			
.gov			
.org			
3-D			
Alignment			
Background/foreground			
Clone			
Color palette			
Crop			
Ctrl+Click			
Data			
Design gallery			
Desk top publishing			
Doc			
Drill down			
Export			
F keys			
Formula			
Handles			
Html			
Hyperlink			
Netiquette			
Network			
Pixels			
Scheme			
Screen shot			
Screen print			
Select-do			
Taskbar			
Toggle			
Tooltip			
Tri-fold			
Washout			
Website address			
WYSIWYG			
Y axis			

Speak Like a Geek Board

Name: _____

Class: _____

WORD DEFINED: _____

Eye contact   _____

Knew word   _____

Knew definition   _____

Used word in sentence   _____

Sentence showed student knew the definition   _____

Audience could help if necessary   _____

Presence   _____

Vocal (no um's, slang, 'something', 'stuff', etc.)   _____

Overall   _____

Lesson #12—Holiday Greetings

Vocabulary	Problem solving	Collaborations
☐ Ctrl ☐ Alt ☐ Template ☐ Placeholder ☐ Link ☐ Forward button ☐ Back button	☐ What if a menu command is grayed-out? (push escape four times) ☐ Can't close a program (Alt+F4) ☐ Can't save (Ctrl+S) ☐ Can't print (Ctrl+P) ☐ My greeting disappeared (insert-text box and put it back in)	☐ Geography ☐ Graphic art
<center>NETS-S: 1.b; 2.b</center>		

Lesson questions? Go to http://askatechteacher.com

Keyboard—Type to Learn/online typing program—good posture; correct hand position

_____ Remember: Goal is 15 wpm by the end of third grade! Speed quiz next week

Lesson Plan—Create a holiday card using Publisher templates. Make it simple (edit text, but don't add new text boxes). Use this lesson to teach templates and design. This project is easy enough to show students how fun and simple computers are.

_____ Open Publisher; find 'Greeting card' templates and select the current holiday. Scroll through the options before selecting. Once one is clicked, select color and font choices on right sidebar and then click 'create'.

_____ Go over card template with students before they begin. Show how pages are on the left sidebar. Explain what 'templates' and 'placeholders' mean

_____ Students can edit text on cover, but don't add new text boxes. Also, have them leave the template formatting in place—don't change fonts, sizes, etc. Students can also change picture by deleting current one and replacing it with insert-clip-art.

_____ Go to page 2; add one or more images (as explained above). Go to page 4 and add name

_____ Save to file folder; print. Show students how to fold card.

Internet practice—if/when student completes card

_____ Go to **www.eduplace.com/geonet/**; extra credit for high score. You may select a different website from the Appendix to go along with classroom inquiry.

Close down to desktop (red X or Alt+F4)

> Bill Gates is a very rich man today... and do you know why? One word: versions.
> — Dave Barry

A snowman grabbed me with one of his stick arms and asked me to tell you something.

Lesson #13—Internet Intro

Vocabulary	Problem solving	Collaborations
☐ *Forward button* ☐ *Back button* ☐ *Links* ☐ *Address* ☐ *Dot* ☐ *'x'*	☐ *I can't exit program (Alt+F4)* ☐ *The screen froze (Is there a dialogue box open?)* ☐ *My document disappeared (check taskbar)*	☐ *Critical thinking* ☐ *Problem solving*
<u>NETS-S:</u> *4. Critical thinking, problem solving, decision making*		

Lesson questions? Go to http://askatechteacher.com

Speed Quiz today—remember the goal of 15 wpm by end of year

____ Good posture; correct hand position, keep eyes on monitor

____ See rules for speed quiz on Lesson #2

Remember: Homework due the end of each month

Vocabulary/Problem solving Review.

____ Problem solving board should be over by now, so it's a good time to remind students of all they learned. Also, review vocab and problems listed above and those encountered during class

____ Take questions from students—what are they having difficulty with; what keyboard shortcuts have they used

Internet practice—www.animatedchristmas.com; www.kidsturncentral.com

____ Type address in independently; be sure to spell correctly and leave no spaces between words or before/after period

____ Explore website; use links, forward and back buttons to get around; be adventurous; don't ask for help unless you're stuck

Option: Those who would like to create a holiday story, see example on next page.

____ This is a good review of the MS Word skills they've already learned.

____ Save and print

Close down to desktop—red X or Alt+F4

Give a person a fish and you feed them for a day; teach a person to use the Internet and they won't bother you for weeks.
— Author Unknown

Holiday Story

Have students write a story. Add a picture in middle and have text wrap around it. Add a border and a WordArt title. Students love this project because it's simple and impressive.

Lesson #14—Google Earth Lats and Longs

Vocabulary	Problem solving	Collaborations
☐ Drill down ☐ Graphic ☐ Network ☐ Text tool	☐ My keyboard won't type (Is the program blinking on the taskbar? Click on it) ☐ How do I print (Ctrl+P)	☐ Vocabulary ☐ Fine motor skills

<u>NETS-S Standards:</u>

6.a

Lesson questions? Go to http://askatechteacher.com

Type to Learn or online typing website—remember: Goal is 15 words per minute

_____ Good posture—keyboard in front of body; sit up straight

_____ Correct hand position—fingers on home row, curved fingers

_____ Remember homework due this month

_____ Focus on keyboard skills—hand position, accuracy, touch typing

Start Speak Like a Geek Board Presentations start today

_____ Review how you'll grade them (use same criteria as Problem Solving Board)

Lesson Plan—Google Earth can be used for many activities. It is a student favorite. Start by reinforcing what they learned in K-2). Remind them how to pan in and out, drag the globe, change earth's perspective. Have them play the built in tour or one you add on a topic they're discussing in class. Finally, ask students to locate major latitudes and longitudes, cities and countries along the lines

_____ Open Google Earth; 'view', 'grid' to activate lats and longs

_____ Point out prominent yellow grid lines—equator, Tropic of Cancer/Capricorn, Arctic/Antarctic Circle, Prime Meridian

_____ Zoom in to see how exact lats and longs get.

_____ Using sheet on next pages, find countries along lats and longs. Do the first one with them so they see how to do it. Students can work in pairs.

_____ Advanced: For those who finish, find the lat and long of their house.

_____ Advanced: For those who finish, give them a lat/long and have them find what's there

_____ Complete sheet—watch for correct spelling!

GOOGLE EARTH LATITUDE/LONGITUDES

Name: _____

Teacher: _____

Find two countries that each of the major lats and longs (latitudes and longitudes) go through:

1. Equator _____

2. Tropic of Cancer_____

3. Arctic Circle_____

4. Tropic of Capricorn_____

5. Antarctic Circle_____

6. Prime meridian_____

7. International date line_____

What country is at N20, E80? _____

What country is S85, E10? _____

Lesson #15—Internet Research

Vocabulary	Problem solving	Collaborations
☐ *Address* ☐ *Copy-paste* ☐ *Plagiarism* ☐ *Extensions* ☐ *Toggle*	☐ *My monitor doesn't work (wake up mouse, check power)* ☐ *My computer doesn't work (check power, check plug)* ☐ *My volume doesn't work (headphones)*	☐ *Spelling* ☐ *Grammar* ☐ *Humanities—cultures* ☐ *Research*
<u>NETS-S Standards:</u> *3.c; 5.a*		

Lesson questions? Go to http://askatechteacher.com

Keyboarding—Type to Learn or online typing site—goal of 15 wpm by end of the year

_____ Good posture; Correct hand position with curved hands

Remember: Homework is due once a month—practice keyboarding at home!

Speak Like a Geek presentations today

Lesson plan— Show students how to research on Google, limit results to the most applicable, then pick the best websites from a list. Apply this knowledge to researching a paper for the classroom

_____ Discuss how to research on the internet—how to recognize a reliable website (extensions), reliable sources (not blogs or chats). Explain the impact of extensions on website reliability.

_____ Discuss the use of limitors—"", +, - in refining hits. Discuss the * as an unknown to answer questions (see inset below).

_____ Set up a MS Word doc to take notes for a classroom project (see next page). Leave it open on taskbar and toggle between these notes and the internet during research; copy-paste text/pictures from the internet to note page.

_____ Discuss 'plagiarism' with students. Remind them to credit sources all the time (copy-paste the website address and the Blue bar site title into their notes)

_____ Walk around as students are researching to guide them through the hits, to the best websites. Explain your decisions.

_____ Go to Google-images and find pictures of the topic

Close down to desk top—red X or Alt+F4

If you type…	You will find pages containing…
Solar system	*Webpages with the words solar and system*
mars OR venus	*Webpages with the word Mars or Venus*
"solar system"	*Webpages with the exact phrase "solar system"*
solar –system	*Webpages with the word solar but NOT system*
"solar system" mars	*Webpages with the phrase "solar system" and Mars*
Fill in the blank	*Use asterisk in sentence and Google will fill it in with the correct information. I.e., 'Mt. Everest is * feet high.*

INDIGENOUS CULTURES—NOTES

1. Native Americans
   "Woods Canyon Pueblo: Life on the Edge"
   http://www.crowcanyon.org/EducationProducts/WOODS/welcome_animation/welcome_new.asp
   2006

Who: The ancient Pueblo people, also known as the Anasazi, lived in the Four Corners region of the Colorado Plateau from 1000 B.C. to A.D. 1300. They built villages of stone, wood, and <u>adobe</u>. Some villages consisted of only a few families, but others had hundreds of people.

2. The Anasazi
   "The Anasazi"
   http://www.desertusa.com/ind1/du_peo_ana.html
   2009

The People of the Mountains, Mesas and Grasslands

| Minerals & Geology | Animals & Wildlife | Plants/ Wildflowers | People & Cultures |

Canyon de Chelly Mummy Cave ruins

Like their cultural kin – the Mogollon and the Hohokam – in the deserts to the south, the earliest Anasazi peoples, felt the currents of revolutionary change during the first half of the first millennium. Perhaps in a response to Mesoamerican influences from <u>Mexico</u>, they began to turn away from the nomadism of the ancient hunting and gathering life, the seasonal rounds calibrated to the movement of game and the ripening of wild plants, the material impoverishment imposed by the limitations of the burdens they could carry on their backs. They began living in small hamlets. They broke the land and took up agriculture. Over time, they acquired more possessions, stored food, made pottery, adopted the bow ...

Research Sites for Grades 3-8

Quick, safe spots to send your students for research:

1. All-around research site libraryspot.com

2. Dictionary www.dictionary.com

3. Edutainment site—requires subscription
   www.brainpop.com/

4. General info research www.infoplease.com/yearbyyear.html

5. Internet research sites for kids
   http://ivyjoy.com/rayne/kidssearch.html

6. Kids search engine for the internet kids.yahoo.com

7. Math, reading, arcade edutainment www.funbrain.com

8. National Geographic for kids kids.nationalgeographic.com/

9. Nova video programs
   www.pbs.org/wgbh/nova/programs.html

10. Research for kids www.factmonster.com/

11. Research—by grade level
    www.iknowthat.com/com/L3?Area=LabelMaps

12. Research—chapters on subjects http://www.worldalmanacforkids.com/

13. Videos on so many topics www.woopid.com/

14. Research—for kids libraryspot.com/

15. Research—history www.infoplease.com/yearbyyear.html

16. School Tube—learning videos from YouTube. Organized by
    topics http://sqooltube.com/

17. Science headlines—audio science.nasa.gov/headlines

18. Search the internet www.google.com

19. Thesaurus—a great one www.thesaurus.com

20. World Book Online (subscription required) www.worldbookonline.com/kids

Lesson #16—Magazine in Publisher I

Vocabulary	Problem solving	Collaborations
☐ *Page parts* ☐ *Text box* ☐ *Desk top publishing* ☐ *Drill down* ☐ *Subtitle*	☐ *My program disappeared (check taskbar)* ☐ *My typing disappeared (Ctrl+Z)*	☐ *Spelling* ☐ *Grammar* ☐ *Humanities* ☐ *History*
	<u>NETS-S:</u> *2.b; 3.c*	

Lesson questions? Go to http://askatechteacher.com

Keyboarding on Type to Learn or online typing site – good posture, hand position
Speak Like a Geek presentations

Lesson Plan—Create a magazine on indigenous cultures (or another topic that correlates with classroom unit of inquiry). Introduce basics of Publisher magazines. Include a cover, table of contents, border, map, banner title, text box, and pictures. Easy start to magazine skills and comes out nicely.

_____ Explain Publisher basics, how it's different from Word and why you'd select it for a project over Word.

_____ Open Publisher and select Quick Publication. Select a template; adjust font/color schemes to fit the topic on the right sidebar; click 'create'

_____ Add title 'Indigenous Cultures'; add student name and teacher as subtitle; replace picture with one of an indigenous people by searching Google Images and copy-pasting to magazine (toggle between tasks on task bar). See sample on next page.

_____ Add five more pages; see them populate on left sidebar

_____ Go to page 2; add Table of Contents (from Page Parts); enlarge to fill page. Heading is 'Table of Contents (font 36, centered); entries are cultural groups (font 18); delete extra rows; add 2 images of cultures at bottom to fill out page

Save to file folder; back-up to flash drive. Close to desk top (X or Alt+F4)

Lesson #17—Magazine in Publisher II

Vocabulary	Problem solving	Collaborations
☐ WordArt ☐ Copy-paste ☐ Save-as ☐ Indigenous ☐ Text box	☐ How do I capitalize (shift for one letter, caps lock for all) ☐ My capital won't go off (Is your caps lock on?)	☐ Spelling ☐ Grammar ☐ Humanities
<div align="center">NETS-S: 2.b; 3.c</div>		

Lesson questions? Go to http://askatechteacher.com

Keyboarding—Type to Learn or online typing website

_____ Good posture; correct hand position, keyboard in front of body

Continue with Speak Like a Geek presentations

Publisher Indigenous Cultures project—2nd of 3 weeks

_____ Open project from file folder; add footer with name and page #. Explain 'footer' to students—when we print, it identifies student, page location

_____ Go to page 3: Add page border; resize to fit just outside of blue print border. Add WordArt title at top for first group; stretch it across as a banner heading, between blue print borders. Add world map (have a .jpg or .gif of a world map in their folder) See insets below.

_____ Copy-paste border, title and map from page 3 to page 4 and 5.

_____ Add text box to page 3. List 5 fast facts about the indigenous culture that students learned in class do the first list with students, as a group. Have them do the rest by themselves.

_____ Add a star to map on each page showing where the page's cultural group is located (i.e., Inca—put star in Peru)

_____ Save to file folder; back-up to flash drive. Ask student why they don't _save-as_.

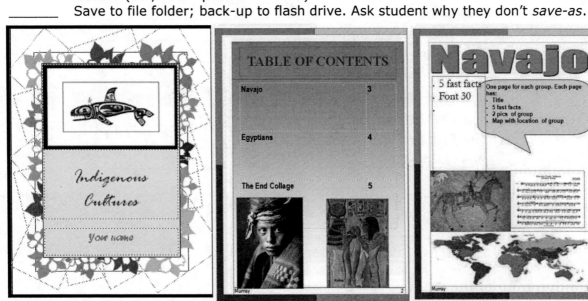

'But I Was Here First'
Grading Rubric

Your name: _____

Teacher: _____

---

1. Title Page   _____ 2 points _____
   a. *Title in large font*   _____
   b. *Your name in smaller font*   _____
   c. *Picture related to topic*   _____

2. Table of Contents   _____ 4 points _____
   a. *Decorative border*   _____
   b. *All topics listed*   _____
   c. *Page numbers match magazine*   _____
   d. *Spell-check, grammar check*   _____
   e. *Extra rows deleted*   _____
   f. *No white space*   _____

3. Magazine Content Pages   _____ 4 points _____
   a. *Border on each page*   _____
   b. *WordArt title at top of page*   _____
   c. *5 fast facts*   _____
   d. *Map with star*   _____
   e. *Two pictures on topic*   _____
   f. *Footer with your name, page*   _____

4. The End Page   4 points
   a. *The End in Word Art*   _____
   b. *The End layered over pictures*   _____
   c. *Picture Collage*   _____

5. Overall Professional Look   _____ 3 points _____

6. Overall Grammar/spelling   _____ 3 points _____

Lesson #18——Magazine in Publisher III

Vocabulary	Problem solving	Collaborations
☐ Borders ☐ Publisher ☐ Collage	☐ I can't find my file folder (check log-in) ☐ Where did my data go? (Ctrl+Z)	☐ Spelling ☐ Grammar ☐ Humanities
<center>NETS-S:</center> <center>2.b; 3.c</center>			

Lesson questions? Go to http://askatechteacher.com

Speak Like a Geek presentations

Publisher—Indigenous Cultures project—final week

_____ Open Publisher with desktop icon; open project

_____ Add 2-3 pictures to fill white space at the bottom of pages 3-5. Images should represent the cultural practices of the group. These can be from Google images or Publisher clipart. Resize as needed to fit available space;

_____ Add collage of pictures to page 6—one from each culture; no white space should remain when finished

_____ Add 'The End' with WordArt to page 6; layer over collage (see inset below)

_____ Check project for accuracy with magazine rubric (see inset below). When completed, submit grading rubric.

_____ As with all projects, if student doesn't d as well as they hoped, they can submit for regarding, for full credit

_____ Save to file folder; save-as to flash drive; print (Ctrl+P)

Keyboarding—Type to Learn or online typing site—for those who finish Publisher project

_____ Good posture—centered in front of keyboard, legs in front

_____ Correct hand position, curved over home row

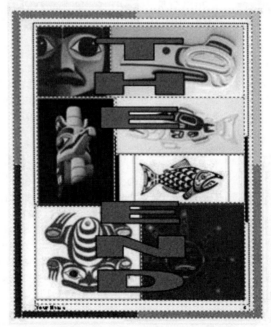

'But I Was Here First'
Grading Rubric

Your name:_____

Teacher:_____

1. Title Page   2 points
   a. Title in large font
   b. Your name in smaller font
   c. Picture related to topic

2. Table of Contents   4 points
   a. Decorative border
   b. All topics listed
   c. Page numbers match magazine
   d. Spell-check, grammar check
   e. Extra rows deleted
   f. No white space

3. Magazine Content Pages   4 points
   a. Border on each page
   b. WordArt title at top of page
   c. 5 fast facts
   d. Map with star
   e. Two pictures on topic
   f. Footer with your name, page

4. The End Page   4 points
   a. The End in Word Art
   b. The End layered over pictures
   c. Picture Collage

5. Overall Professional Look   3 points

6. Overall Grammar/spelling   3 points

Lesson #19—Introduction to Excel I

Vocabulary	Problem solving	Collaborations
☐ Cells ☐ Rows ☐ Columns ☐ X axis ☐ Y axis ☐ Data ☐ Worksheet	☐ *I can't find my file folder (check log-in. Are you in correct name?)* ☐ *My graph is empty (Did you highlight data before pushing F11?)* ☐ *Where did my data go (Press Ctrl+Z to undo)*	☐ Spelling ☐ Grammar ☐ Math
	<u>NETS-S:</u> *3.b; 4.c*	

Lesson questions? Go to http://askatechteacher.com

Keyboarding—Type to Learn or online typing website—remember good posture; hands curved over home row

Speak Like a Geek presentations

Lesson Plan— In this math lesson, students conduct a random survey and use Excel to create a bar graph of results. Students learn not only how to input data, but turn it into information in a few quick steps. They're always amazed how easy it is to look like a pro.

_____ Explain basics of Excel—columns, rows, cells, how cells named

_____ Double-click 'sheet 1' tab; rename 'Subjects'; right click tab to change color

_____ Project the sample on next page on classroom screen or SmartBoard. Students will add data in cells shown on sample.

_____ Add table name, student name, date, column headings, subjects in cells indicated

_____ Collect data on class's favorite subject divided by boys and girls; each student gets only one vote; highlight data from a5 to c9 (all labels, titles and data) and push F11 to graph.

_____ Discuss with students the difference between seeing raw data on the spreadsheet and the filtered data on the chart. Most people prefer the colorful chart, but it has shortfalls: It's conclusions make it hard to see anything else about the data. This stops people from drawing their own conclusions. With raw data, people are more encouraged to study the numbers and draw their own unique conclusions. Do students see anything on the spreadsheet that isn't communicated on the chart?

_____ Notice that the chart opened up on a new worksheet. Double-click new worksheet tab; rename 'subjects chart'

_____ Right-click chart; go to 'format chart'; add title, x and y labels

_____ Advanced: Right-click chart; format chart area /plot area; Change background and colors. Be sure the formatting doesn't interfere with the readers' ability to see the numbers.

_____ Ctrl+S to save; save-as to flash drive; print (Ctrl+P). Why do students save once and then save-as the second time?

Close down to desk top (X or Alt+F4)

What Is Your Favorite Subject?

By Brandon

1/25/2005

	A	B	C
5	**Subject**	**boys**	**girls**
6	Math	2	1
7	Science	1	1
8	Art	5	7
9	Computers	2	0

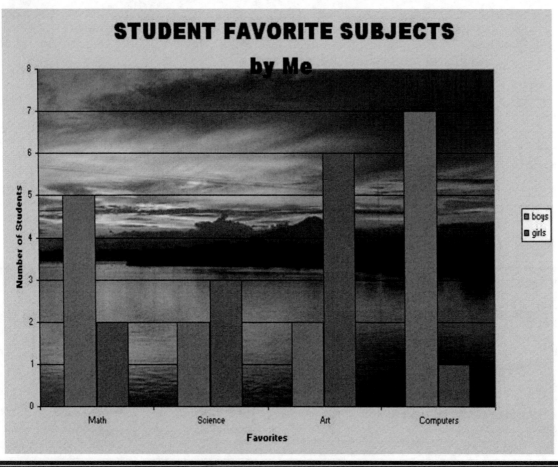

STUDENT FAVORITE SUBJECTS
by Me

Lesson #20—Introduction to Excel II

Vocabulary	Problem solving	Collaborations
☐ Graph ☐ Formula ☐ Cells ☐ Rows ☐ Columns	☐ I entered my data in the wrong cell (highlight the cell; drag-and-drop to the correct spot) ☐ My column is too small (double click between the columns to resize)	☐ Math ☐ Critical thinking ☐ Problem solving skills

NETS-S
3.b; 4.c

Lesson questions? Go to http://askatechteacher.com

Keyboard—Type to Learn or online typing website—correct posture—body centered in front of computer; correct hand position—curved over home row

Speak Like a Geek—continue presentations—finish in 2-3 weeks

Lesson Plan—Show students how to use Excel formulas to add, subtract, multiply and divide. Have students practice with worksheets provided by the classroom teacher. They can first figure out the answers themselves and then check them against Excel's formulas. My students love this!

_____ Use student interest in math to create a study guide with formulas

_____ Open Excel—open project saved last week. Have students use this workbook for all Excel projects—just add new tabs

_____ Double-click worksheet tab; rename it 'Math'; right-click and change 'tab color'

_____ Go to A1—put title for spreadsheet, "Auto Math"

_____ Go to A2—put your name

_____ Go to A3—add subtitle 'Addition'; click row '3' and color with paint bucket

_____ Use teacher-supplied sample worksheet to add math problems

_____ Highlight and use Excel formula to add (=b4+b5). Use the easy way—*equal sign; click the first cell; add the function; click the second cell; enter*

_____ Finish all problems on worksheet in similar fashion using formulas (+=add; -=subtract; *=multiply; /=divide)

_____ Have students replace some of the numbers to see how answers change. This is a true WOW event—they love it!

_____ Save; save-as to flash drive; close to desktop

	A	B	C	D	E	F	G
1			AUTO MATH				
2	Your Name						
3	Addition						
4			99	144	720	1044	2583
5			33	12	20	132	357
6		Total	132	156			
7							
8	Subtraction						
9			35682	144	720	1044	2583
10			29876	12	20	132	357
11		Total	5806				
12							
13	Multiplication						
14			99	144	720	1044	2583
15			33	12	20	132	357
16			3267	1728			

You know you're a geek when you can do hexadecimal arithmetic in your head.

AUTO MATH

	A	B	C	D	E	F	G
1							
2	Your Name						
3	Addition						
4			99	144	720	1044	2583
5			33	12	20	132	357
6		Total	132	156			
7							
8	Subtraction						
9			35682	144	720	1044	2583
10			29876	12	20	132	357
11		Total	5806				
12							
13	Multiplication						
14			99	144	720	1044	2583
15			33	12	20	132	357
16			3267	1728			

Lesson #21—Introduction to Excel III

Vocabulary	Problem solving	Collaborations
☐ Internet ☐ Address ☐ Favorites ☐ Excel formula ☐ Tab ☐ Internet address ☐ Back button	☐ My program disappeared (check taskbar) ☐ The link doesn't work (copy-paste it into address bar on browser) ☐ I can't remember the address (did you save to Favorites?)	☐ Math ☐ Humanities
NETS-S:		
4.b, 4.c		

Lesson questions? Go to http://askatechteacher.com

Keyboard—Type to Learn or online typing site

_____ Correct posture—centered in front of computer, hands curved over home row

Remember: Homework due the end of each month

Speak Like a Geek—almost finished

Excel project—3rd of 3 weeks

_____ Open saved project; go to worksheet tab named 'Auto Math'

_____ Remember: + = add; - = subtract; * = multiply; / = divide

_____ Finish Auto Math worksheet started last week; replace some numbers and see how it recalculates; click in the cell for the answer and notice the cell contents—it's a formula, not a number

_____ When done, save. Why did you 'save' and not 'save-as'? Close to desktop

Internet—for those finished with worksheet

_____ Select several math websites from list in the Appendix and put them on the class internet start page. Students who have finished with Excel can visit any of these websites and practice their math skills

_____ Explore; use back button and forward button to get around; try different links

_____ Go to another on the list if you have time

_____ Save all sites visited to 'Favorites'

_____ Close internet with 'x'

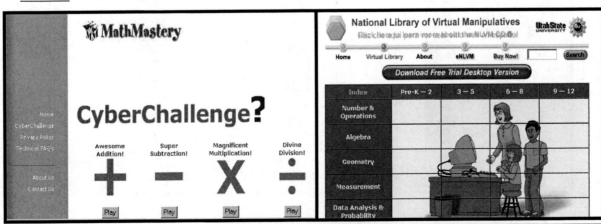

Lesson #22—ASCII Art

Vocabulary	Problem solving	Collaborations
☐ ASCII ☐ Geek ☐ Toggle ☐ Watermark	☐ My keypad doesn't work (push 'Num Lock' key) ☐ Some math problems take too long (use tab key to move between fields)	☐ Math ☐ Humanities
	NETS-S: *3.b, 3.c*	

Lesson questions? Go to http://askatechteacher.com

Keyboard—Type to Learn—correct posture, correct hand position
Speak Like a Geek—finish last of presentation
Sign up for Google Earth Board Presentations—start next week

_____ Students select a date to present and a location from a list of places they visited during third grade, the Wonders of the World, or ???. I've included the list my classes used last year for examples.

_____ Use research skills learned in Lesson #15 to find one Fascinating Fact about that location to share with classmates. Allow students to skip a 45-minute homework to give them 45 minutes to do their research.

_____ Fill out all information on the study guide (see next pages), including Fascinating Fact.

_____ Grading will be based on criteria listed on the grading rubric (see next pages)

Lesson Plan—ASCII Art. This is drawing with letters and numbers for fun and as another way to excite students about keyboarding

_____ Have students sign up for the Google Earth Board while working on their ASCII Art drawing

_____ Add a watermark of a picture you like to a Word doc, preferably a single image (see below). Type over the drawing with letters or numbers (if you're more patient than I, you can pick a variety of letters. That would provide more depth). When typing completely covers the image, select different parts and color the digits, i.e., I colored the x's on the pumpkin's stem green.

_____ When done, delete the watermark. Looks good, huh?

_____ Save and print

GOOGLE EARTH BOARD SIGN-UP

	Teacher A	B	C
Week of Dec. 15th			
Week of Jan. 5th			
Week of Jan. 12th			
Week of Jan. 19th			
Week of Jan 26th			
Week of Feb. 2nd			
Week of Feb. 9th			
Week of Feb. 23rd			
Week of Mar. 2nd			

Pick a Location:	Class A	B	C
Egyptian Pyramids			
Great Wall of China			
Stonehenge			
Hagia Sophia, Istanbul			
Leaning Tower of Pisa			
The Eiffel Tower			
Panama Canal			
Taj Mahal			
Victoria Falls			
Ngorongoro Crater			
Mt. Everest			
Ayers Rock			
The Ross Ice Shelf			
Tierra del Fuego			
Straits of Gibraltar			
The Red Sea			
Mt. St. Helens			
San Andreas Fault			
Great African Rift			
Madagascar			
Istanbul			
Siberia			
Death Valley			
Suez Canal			
Vatican City			
The Chunnel			

GOOGLE EARTH BOARD PROJECT

Your name:_____

Your Teacher_____

Estimated time: 45 minutes

1. Write your Google Earth Board location here:_____
2. Write the date of your class presentation here:_____
3. Find your location on Google Earth
4. Print a picture of your location from Google Earth and paste it here:

5. Look up one interesting fact about this location and write it here:

_____

_____

_____

6. When you make your presentation, turn this sheet in to me, filled out
7. Grading will be based on:
    a. Were you prepared on the correct date:
    b. Did you have a picture:
    c. Did you have an interesting fact:
    d. Did you speak loud enough for seat 19 to hear:
    e. Did you avoid 'umms', etc
    f. Did you look the audience in the eye as you talked:
8. You may skip a homework. Put the number of the one you are skipping here:_____

Notes:

- Type the location name in as it is written on the Google Earth Board. That is your best chance of finding it

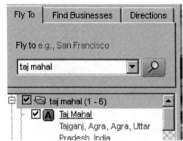

- Turn off the markers for community notations (the check box that comes up under the 'fly to' locations) before saving the picture

- Save picture as 'file—save—save image' and then select your flash drive

- Turn your 3D buildings on (under 'layers')

- Be sure to pan in so we can clearly see your

location or building

- You can get the interesting fact from the encyclopedia, Wikipedia, your parents, or something you learned in class

- If you can't find a location, try the Google Earth Community for a link (for example, use the Community for Ross Ice Shelf)

- If you know the location, you may go there without using the 'fly to' option; just add your own place marker (this might work better for 'San Andreas Fault' and the 'Great African Rift')

GOOGLE EARTH BOARD GRADING

Name: _____

Class: _____

You were prepared with filled-out project sheet _____

Your project sheet had a picture of your location _____

You shared an interested fact with the class _____

You spoke loudly enough for all to hear _____

You seemed knowledgeable _____

You had a calm, confident presence _____

You didn't use vocal cues that showed nervousness_____

You didn't use visual cues that showed nervousness_____

You looked your audience in the eye as you talked _____

Overall impression _____

Lesson #23—Creating Computer Wallpaper

Vocabulary	Problem solving	Collaborations
☐ Text tool ☐ Paint tool ☐ Tool bar ☐ .org	☐ The website toolbar at the top disappeared (Press F11) ☐ I can't read the website text (Ctrl++ to zoom in)	☐ Science ☐ Art ☐ Human body
NETS-S: 1.b, 3.b		

Lesson questions? Go to http://askatechteacher.com

Keyboard—Type to Learn—correct posture (centered, legs in front)

_____ Correct hand position—both hands on home row, curved

Google Earth presentations start today

Lesson Plan— Kids love personalizing their computer stations. Show them how to create their own wallpaper using internet pictures, pictures on the computer or their own photos or drawings. There are five ways (see samples on next page):

_____ One: Right click on Windows desktop; go to 'personalize', 'desktop background' and pick one. Depending upon your version of Windows, this may differ slightly.

_____ Two: Go to your 'Pictures' folder on your computer; right click on the picture you like and select 'set as desktop background'

_____ Three: Go to one of the many wallpaper websites ('wallpaper' is another term for 'desktop background') and download one of theirs. Try National Geographic—they have beautiful nature wallpapers.

_____ Four: Go to the internet; right click on a picture you like and select 'set as desktop background'

_____ Five: Create your own in KidPix (or Paint). Students may do that with the remainder of class

Those who prefer may make a holiday card for a family member without help in KidPix.

_____ This project uses skills they have mastered in the past

_____ Suggest text tool, paint tool, paint bucket

_____ Save and print; close down to desktop

Advanced: Make this the wallpaper for the student's station.

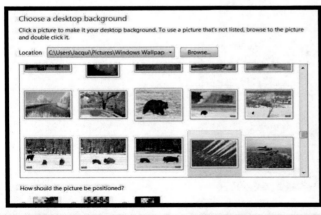

Lesson #24—PowerPoint I

Vocabulary	Problem solving	Collaborations
☐ Slideshow ☐ Task pane ☐ Place saver ☐ Text box ☐ Bullets ☐ Tool bar	☐ How do I insert a slide (use 'New Slide' tool on the toolbar) ☐ My bullets disappeared (Push the bullet tool on the toolbar) ☐ My text box disappeared (Insert-text box from menu bar)	☐ Grammar ☐ Spelling ☐ Understanding and applying information
NETS-S: 2.b, 4.b		

Lesson questions? Go to http://askatechteacher.com

Keyboard—Type to Learn or online typing website—correct posture

_____ Correct hand position—both hands on home row, curved over keys

Google Earth Board—continue with presentations

Lesson Plan—Have students share their favorite colors, foods, holidays, etc. Or, link to a topic being discussed in class (i.e., types of government). Use this project to review all PowerPoint basics learned in 2nd grade—adding slides/text/pictures, animation, transitions, clipart, internet pictures, auto-advance. Have each students present when completed to practice the unique skills of presentations using PowerPoint.

_____ Introduce PowerPoint—its purpose, how it's different from Word, the basics

_____ Show samples from last year. This always excites students.

_____ Open PowerPoint using Start button, icon, to blank slideshow

_____ Discuss program layout—slides on the left, slide they're working on in middle

_____ Add 9 slides. Watch them populate on left. Click Slide #1 and add title—'My Favorites'; Click to add subtitle—your name and teacher (see inset below)

_____ Slide 2: Table of Contents—add entire list (see inset below). Use bullet list—capitalize each bullet; push enter to add new bullet

_____ Advanced: Add a bar graphic-animated gif—to each slide, between title and contents (see sample below)

_____ Slide 3 through 9—title at top of each from Table of Contents

_____ Slide 10—The End in WordArt

_____ Save to your file folder—lastname 3 ss; close down to desktop

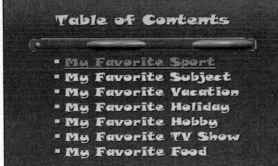

Lesson #25—PowerPoint II

Vocabulary	Problem solving	Collaborations
☐ PowerPoint ☐ Slideshow ☐ Slide ☐ GIF ☐ Movie ☐ Background ☐ Heading	☐ Shift doesn't work (turn caps lock off) ☐ How do I make the picture move? (Play slideshow) ☐ How do I know which title goes on which slide (It must match the Table of Contents order)	☐ Grammar ☐ Spelling
	NETS-S: *2.b, 4.b*	

Lesson questions? Go to http://askatechteacher.com

Keyboard—Type to Learn or online typing site

_____ Correct posture—body centered in front of keyboard, elbows at sides

_____ Correct hand position—both hands curved over home row

Remember: Homework due the end of each month

Continue Google Earth Board presentations

Continue PowerPoint slideshow project

_____ Open project saved last week

_____ If you haven't finished titles and title bar, finish that

_____ Show slide sample—each slide will have 4 parts (see sample below)

_____ Slide 3 through 9 will correspond to the Table of Contents. Enter the titles in the same order and always capitalize the first letter of each word in heading

_____ Slide 3-9: Add a full sentence Explaining what your favorite *** is and why. Watch grammar and spelling, punctuation and capitals

_____ Don't worry about pictures yet. Let's get the typing done first.

_____ Save to your file folder—lastname 3 ss; close down to desktop

She's trying Ctrl+U

Lesson #26—PowerPoint III

Vocabulary	Problem solving	Collaborations
☐ *Ribbon* ☐ *Slide* ☐ *Right-click* ☐ *Animation* ☐ *Scheme*	☐ *I can't find my project (go to Start button, search)* ☐ *The computer didn't save my project (Check your back-up or My Documents?)*	☐ *Grammar* ☐ *Spelling* ☐ *Critical thinking skills*
<div align="center">**NETS-S:** *2.b, 4.b*</div>		

Lesson questions? Go to http://askatechteacher.com

Keyboard—Type to Learn or online typing website (see appendix for suggestions)—correct posture—keyboard centered in front of body

Google Earth Board—continue presentations

Continue PowerPoint slideshow project—week 3 of 5

_____ Open project saved last week

_____ Finish sentences for each of your favorites—capitalize first letter, period at the end; good grammar and spelling

_____ Go to Slide #1; Click 'Design' on menu bar. Pick a background that fits the topic and select it. Notice all slides change to that background

_____ But, we want at least three slides to have different backgrounds. Here's how you do that: Select a background you like and right-click it. Select 'Add to selected slide' from the drop-down menu

_____ Time to add movement. Only animate the titles. Discuss the word 'animate' with students. What does that mean? Go to Slide #1; select the title. Go to 'animation' on menu bar and select an animation from 'entrance' or 'emphasis'—not exit. Animate the title of each slide

_____ Time to add pictures. Pictures can be static or moving—discuss the difference. PowerPoint calls the moving ones 'movies' but sometimes they're called 'animated gifs'.

_____ Go to Slide #1; add two pictures, one moving and one static. Use clipart or Google images for static. Use 'movies' for other. Show students how to tell the difference (movies have a star in the lower right corner). Make sure image matches text.

_____ Save. Why do we 'save' and not 'save-as'? Close down to desktop

Problem solving: If your screen freezes:
"Enter any 11-digit prime number to continue..."

Lesson #27—PowerPoint IV

Vocabulary	Problem solving	Collaborations
☐ Multimedia ☐ PowerPoint ☐ Slide show ☐ Auto advance ☐ Transition ☐ GIF	☐ Program disappeared (check taskbar) ☐ My animated GIF doesn't move (play slideshow and you'll see it) ☐ I don't like the picture I picked (click to select and push 'delete' to remove ☐ I can't play one slide (use shift+F5)	☐ Grammar ☐ Spelling
NETS-S:		
2.b, 4.b		

Lesson questions? Go to http://askatechteacher.com

Type to Learn or online typing website—body centered in front of keyboard, elbows at sides

_____ Correct hand position—hands curved over home row

Continue Google Earth presentations

Remember: Homework due the end of each month

Continue PowerPoint slideshow project—week 4 of 5

_____ Open project saved last week. If students can't find theirs, go to 'My Documents'—that's a common mistake. Not there? Use Search function.

_____ Go to Slide #1; select 'transition' from menu bar. Discuss what 'transition' means with students. What's the prefix –trans? What are other trans- words? Select a transition you like. Once you select a transition, it is on the slide until you change it

_____ Before leaving this slide, go to right end of ribbon, and check box for 'after'; make it 5 seconds. This will cause the slideshow to auto-advance without anyone having to click the mouse

_____ Optional: Add sound to slide.

_____ Repeat these steps for each slide, with a different transition

_____ Push F5 to test slideshow. Does it auto-advance? If not, go into the slide where it stopped; check to be sure you have the transition auto-advanced. If that's OK, go to 'animation'; select the title you animated and have it start 'with previous'. That should fix the problem. Use Shift+F5 to start from a particular slide rather than from the beginning.

_____ Save (not save-as)

Lesson #28—PowerPoint V

Vocabulary	Problem solving	Collaborations
☐ Tool bar ☐ Drill down ☐ Task pane ☐ Design	☐ My picture got weird (only use corner handles) ☐ What's wpm? (Words per minute—divide your total by five)	☐ Grammar ☐ Spelling
NETS-S: 2.b, 4.b		

Lesson questions? Go to http://askatechteacher.com

Type to Learn or online typing site—correct hand position—curved over home row

Speed quiz—see rules for speed quiz on Lesson #2. Remember: Don't correct spelling/grammar mistakes during test. There'll be one minute to correct after buzzer.

_____ Open Word; place sheet next to keyboard (see samples on Lesson #2)

_____ Heading at top; type for 5 minutes, then spell check with right click on red squiggly lines

_____ Type word count at bottom of sheet (divide by 5 for wpm)

_____ Save (why aren't you using 'save-as'?); print for me

_____ Close down to desktop

Google Earth Board—continue presentations

Continue PowerPoint slideshow project—week 5 of 5

_____ Open project saved last week

_____ Add footer to slideshow with student name and slide #

_____ Tasks not completed can be finished during this period—headings, animations, transitions, gif's, footer

_____ When done, complete grading rubric/check list (see next page)

_____ Turn rubric in. Presentations start next week. Presentations include eye contact, no umms, no slang (see check list)

_____ Do practice run—F5 to start slideshow; go through your speech. Match speed of slideshow with speed of presentation

Done? Go to any websites on class internet start page (or have a group of websites that apply to what students are working on in the classroom

Close down to desktop (red 'x' or Alt+F4)

"See Daddy! All the keys are in alphabetical order now!"

The End

Good Bye!!!

POWERPOINT GRADING RUBRIC

Name_____   Teacher_____

Here's a list of skills required in your PowerPoint project. Check off those that you've included. Then, add those that you've missed. When you're done, turn in the grading rubric and I'll grade your project.

1. Title slide   _____

2. Table of Contents   _____

3. The end slide   _____

4. Each slide has title   _____

5. Each slide has sentence of favorite   _____

6. Each slide has picture   _____

7. Each slide has GIF   _____

8. No spelling/grammar errors   _____

9. 5 animations   _____

10. 5 transitions   _____

11. 5 sounds   _____

12. Slides auto-advance   _____

13. Class presentation   _____

    a. Face audience   _____

    b. Talk to audience   _____

    c. Introduce yourself and topic   _____

    d. Speak loud enough   _____

    e. No 'umms' or stuttering   _____

Lesson #29—Book Report in Word I

Vocabulary	Problem solving	Collaborations
☐ *Center* ☐ *Page break* ☐ *Ctrl+enter* ☐ *Auto-play* ☐ *Center tool* ☐ *Cover page*	☐ *How do I capitalize? (shift for one letter, caps lock for all)* ☐ *My program's gone (check taskbar)* ☐ *How do I make a new page (Ctrl+enter at the bottom of the previous page)*	☐ *Grammar* ☐ *Spelling.* ☐ *Composition*
<u>NETS-S:</u> *2.b, 4.b*		

Lesson questions? Go to http://askatechteacher.com

Google Earth Board presentations—almost done

Begin typing Word book report

_____ Cover page—center name, author, publisher, illustrator, your name, teacher, date

_____ Use print-preview to check the layout; center text vertically on page

_____ Ctrl+Enter at bottom of page to start a new page

_____ Change font to 14, Times New Roman. Center titles and underline, left-align paragraphs, tab to indent paragraphs (see samples on next pages)

_____ Spell-check and grammar-check

PowerPoint slideshow presentations—do this as a break from typing

_____ Open student slideshow on classroom monitor or SmartBoard; dim lights

_____ Student can have notes, but shouldn't read them. They know about themselves so shouldn't need to read from the screen either

_____ Student should keep their presentation to the five-seconds allowed by the auto-play they put in under 'transition'

_____ Audience should pay attention, not fidget, and be polite

_____ Presentations include eye contact, no umms, no slang, speak loudly

Students can take up to three questions after their presentation. These should be positive questions, asking to expand on some item included in the slideshow, not asking why the presenter made a mistake (if they did), and not pointing out shortfalls. Have audience applaud at the end.

<u>A LONG WAY FROM CHICAGO</u>

Author: Richard Peck

Publisher: Scholastic

Illustrator: Debora Smith

MY FAVORITE THINGS

By Your Name

CLASSROOM BOOK REPORT TEMPLATE

TITLE
(Bold, caps, 36 font)

Author
Publisher
Illustrator

Your name
Your Teacher
Date

Major Characters

Indent first line. Type at least five sentences in each paragraph. Double space between sections.

Setting

Indent first line. Type at least five sentences in each paragraph. Double space between sections.

Summary

Indent first line. Type at least five sentences in each paragraph. Double space between sections.

My Favorite Part

Indent first line. Type at least five sentences in each paragraph. Double space between sections.

Add footer with your name and page number.

Lesson #30— Book Report in Word II

Vocabulary	Problem solving	Collaborations
☐ Auto-advance ☐ Transition ☐ Animation ☐ Sentence fragment	☐ My computer doesn't work (is power on?) ☐ My monitor doesn't work (is power on?)	☐ Spelling ☐ Grammar ☐ Composition
NETS-S: *3.c, 4.c*		

Lesson questions? Go to http://askatechteacher.com

Finish Google Earth Board presentations

Type Word book report

_____ Cover page—center name, author, publisher, illustrator, your name, teacher, due date

_____ Use print-preview and enter key to center title page material on page

_____ Ctrl+Enter to start a new page (make sure student is at the bottom of the page when they push Ctrl+Enter); double-space the rest of the report using the ribbon tool

_____ Change font to 14, non-bold, Times New Roman, for rest of the report (not cover)

_____ Center titles, left-align paragraphs, tab to indent paragraphs

_____ Spell-check and grammar-check, capitalize proper nouns

_____ Capitalize first letter of sentence, period at end, space between words; allow Word to wrap to new line. Students will try to push enter to move down to a new line—don't let them. Use the show/hide tool to check this. Explain why this doesn't work and show them how to fix it.

_____ As students finish each section, have them fix all sentence fragments—is there a subject and verb?

PowerPoint slideshow presentations—again, use this as a break from typing

_____ Open student slideshow on classroom screen

_____ Student will not have hardcopy of slideshow so have him/her stand where s/he can see the screen or SmartBoard

_____ Student presentation should stay on time with auto-play of slides

_____ Audience should pay attention, not fidget, be polite

_____ Presentations include eye contact, no umms, no slang

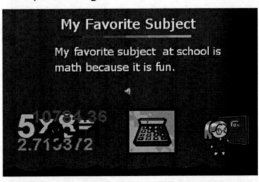

Lesson #31——Oregon Trail I

Vocabulary	Problem solving	Collaborations
☐ *GIF* ☐ *Movie* ☐ *Shift+F5* ☐ *Esc* ☐ *Download* ☐ *Ctrl+click* ☐ *Tab-indent*	☐ *Screen froze (Is a dialogue box open?)* ☐ *How do I use a link in a document (Ctrl+click)* ☐ *What are those red squiggly lines? (Spelling errors. Right-click and select correct spelling)*	☐ *Grammar* ☐ *Spelling, etc.* ☐ *Humanities* ☐ *History*
<u>NETS-S:</u> *3.b, 4.a*		

Lesson questions? Go to http://askatechteacher.com

PowerPoint slideshow presentations

_____ Open student slideshow on classroom TV

_____ Student will not have hardcopy of slideshow—stand where s/he can see screen; be sure to match presentation with auto-play timing

_____ Audience should pay attention, not fidget, be polite

_____ Presentations include eye contact, no umms, no slang

Lesson Plan—Use Oregon Trail to collaborate with classroom discussion on westward expansion. Show students how to get the most out of this simulation by reading the headings on each screen, thinking about problem solving skills and applying the simulation to their reservoir of knowledge on this topic. I include a worksheet of questions for them to answer as well as additional websites to extend their exploration. If your Oregon Trail doesn't run well on Windows (like mine doesn't), teach problem solving skills to turn a difficulty into a teaching moment.

This week, open Oregon Trail from the beginning so students learn about selecting supplies. Next week, have them use 'Quick Start'.

Download 'Oregon Trail' Word doc from network file folder (where you've put it). Save-as to student file folder. (see Word doc on next pages)

As students play the simulation, toggle between questions and game to type answers to questions into Word doc (explain how they should use 'over-type' on the 'insert' key)

If the program freezes (it doesn't play well with Win7 in my school), teach students **Alt+F4, Ctr+Alt+Del, Task Manager** to solve problems. If Oregon Trail hides, use **Alt+tab** to cycle through open screens. If it collapses to the taskbar, **check the taskbar** for open programs, Sound difficult? Not for students excited to be playing this game.

_____ Can't find answers in the game? Teach students how to use Ctrl+click to use links on links page (page 2 of the questionnaire)—no need to retype

_____ When time is up, close without saving. Even if students save, the next class will save over them. Next week, they'll start over, but this time with Quick Start—that puts them on the trail.

OREGON TRAIL

*Your Name:*_____

*Your teacher:*_____

As you play "Oregon Trail", fill the form in below with answers to the questions:

1. Name two states the Oregon Trail crossed through.
    a. _____
    b. _____

2. Name two reasons settlers headed out on the Oregon Trail?
    a. _____
    b. _____

3. Describe a covered wagon

    _____

4. Describe five supplies it carried.
    a. _____   d. _____
    b. _____   e. _____
    c. _____

5. Describe two landmarks they encountered
    a. _____
    b. _____

6. List two hardships they faced
    a. _____
    b. _____

7. List two diseases they faced.
    a. _____
    b. _____

8. List two types of weather they encountered?
    a. _____
    b. _____

9. List two mistakes they made on the trail?
    a. _____
    b. _____

10. How did they solve problems on the trail?
    a. _____
    b. _____

How to Teach Problem-solving With Oregon Trail and Win7

My students love <u>Oregon Trail</u>. It fits nicely with a unit of inquiry in both 3rd and 4th grade. *Oregon Trail* makes it easy to catch the important concepts because it puts them right at the top of the screen–*You die of malaria, You reach the Blue River*. I ask questions of students like *What were problems faced by settlers along the trail* (they caught diseases)? *What natural landmarks did they cross* (the Blue River). I have 3rd graders fill out a questionnaire and I have 4th graders complete an expanded version digitally. They bring a Word doc up electronically and fill it out on the computer as they play the game.

This two-week unit is a big hit with students. Here's the problem. Oregon Trail doesn't play well with Win 7. It freezes, stalls, blows up. We've called the manufacturer, but no luck. At first, I was sorely disappointed to lose such a valuable simulation. All of the 'trail' series are wonderful–Amazon Trail, Inca Trail, Yukon Trail. The only one that is networked is Oregon Trail, so I limited myself to that one, not wanting the confusion of CD's popping in and out of drives and getting scratched and broken.

Then I had an epiphany as I watched students work through the stalls and freezes. They wanted to know how to fix the problems so they could continue with the game. Wow. What better way to teach problem solving than to teach it with real-life situations that students are motivated to solve. It's turned into a successful problem-solving lesson.

Here's what we learn:

- When the program freezes, they learn that **Alt+F4** will close down programs most of the time so they can restart
- If Alt+F4 doesn't work, they learn how to get to the **Task Manager with Ctr+Alt+Del.**
- They learn that once in the task manager, they go to **'applications', select the offending program and click 'end task'**. All of us have had to do that. Now the kids know how
- Sometimes, Oregon Trail is hidden behind a black screen. Students learn to use **Alt+tab** to cycle through open screens
- Sometimes, the program collapses to the taskbar. Students learn to **check the taskbar** for open programs, click on the one they want and re-open

Problem solving is an important part of technology. Computers never go smoothly and progressing past these speed bumps is the most frustrating part of working with tech. Through this lesson, students learn that it's part of life, that problems can be solved, and they accept them without the drama of throwing the computer away and starting over.

I will probably continue with this program next year, with an introduction that they aren't just learning about settlers.

Lesson #32——Oregon Trail II

Vocabulary	Problem solving	Collaborations
■ *Download* ■ *Overtype* ■ *Links* ■ *Task manager*	■ *I can't get out of town (use the Quick Start option)* ■ *My program froze (use Alt+F4 or Ctr+Alt+Del)*	☐ *Spelling* ☐ *Grammar* ☐ *Humanities* ☐ *History*
<u>NETS-S:</u> *3.b, 4.1*		

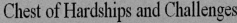

Lesson questions? Go to <u>http://askatechteacher.com</u>

PowerPoint slideshow presentations

_____ Open student slideshow on classroom screen or SmartBoard

_____ Stand where s/he has clear view of their slideshow

_____ Stay with auto-play speed of presentation

_____ Audience should pay attention, not fidget

Lesson Plan—teach problem solving while using Oregon Trail. Problem solving is an important part of technology. Computers never go smoothly and progressing past these speed bumps is the most frustrating part of working with tech. Through this lesson, students learn that it's part of life, that problems can be solved, and they accept them without the drama of throwing the computer away and starting over

_____ Open 'Oregon Trail' and the questionnaire (from student's network file folder).

_____ Type answers found in Oregon Trail directly onto the questionnaire—use 'overtype' (insert key)

_____ Can't find the answer in Oregon Trail? Answer questions using knowledge from class simulation or links on page 2. **Use Ctrl+click** to access links in Word doc. This is a new skill in third grade. Students not only learn to use embedded links, but to **complete a Word doc on the computer**.

_____ When Oregon Trail freezes, use problem solving skills (see prior lesson – Alt+F4, Ctrl+Alt+Del, Task Manager, check task bar)

_____ When questionnaire is completed, print only page 1 (not the other pages). Students learn to print by page rather than document.

_____ Students can collaborate with each other on answers.

_____ Walk around and help students think through this variety of problem-solving experiences

HOMEWORK #3-1—via email

HOMEWORK	GRADE

Send me an email from home with:

- Your name
- Your email address
- Your parents' names
- What you want to learn about computers
- What you know about computers

Email Subject Line: 'last name Grade Homework

Submitted: 5 pts
Late: -1
Not submitted: 0 pts

Don't take more than 45 minutes!!

HOMEWORK #3-2—via email

HOMEWORK	GRADE
The hints below are from prior year's Third Graders to help you get the most out of this year. Read them and then type five of your favorites into an email and send them to me. Stop after 45 minutes.	Submitted: 5 pts Subject line protocol: -1. Late: -1 Not submitted: 0 pts

Hints for Incoming Third Graders
Collected from last year's third graders

Hard things/Things I don't like

- ☐ Speed quizzes, especially timed
- ☐ Catching up on homework
- ☐ Homework, especially typing
- ☐ A report about myself—difficult
- ☐ Learning where the letters are
- ☐ MS Publisher, Excel
- ☐ Vocabulary quizzes
- ☐ Typing the book report on Word
- ☐ Getting to websites
- ☐ Using all my fingers when typing
- ☐ Getting a 100% on typing tests
- ☐ The Publisher report was hard

Easy things/My Favorite things

- ☐ Making and presenting slideshows
- ☐ Help me do repetitive things like copy and paste
- ☐ Email
- ☐ This is one of my favorite classes
- ☐ Making cards for other people
- ☐ PowerPoint—for class projects
- ☐ MS Word, Publisher—easy and fun
- ☐ Learning to double space and spell-check in Word
- ☐ Getting to do work over that you didn't do well on
- ☐ Type to Learn
- ☐ The games, internet, Word, PowerPoint
- ☐ Magic School Bus, KidPix, Clipart
- ☐ Learning things that are going on in the world
- ☐ Fixing mistakes without an eraser
- ☐ Learning things we use the rest of our lives

Advice

- ☐ Do your homework
- ☐ Listen in class
- ☐ Don't be afraid to ask questions
- ☐ No internet w/o permission
- ☐ Get extra credit if you need it
- ☐ Practice typing
- ☐ If you can't do homework, get a FREE
- ☐ Don't put your hand up when the teacher is talking
- ☐ Do lots of practice and do your homework
- ☐ Have fun
- ☐ Don't goof off or you get in trouble
- ☐ Memorize keyboard so speed quizzes are easy
- ☐ Follow directions; be patient with instruction
- ☐ Try hard, turn homework in on time, have fun
- ☐ Learn to make columns
- ☐ Save often
- ☐ Don't fear computer—you can't break it!
- ☐ Learn to take care of the computers
- ☐ Don't use slang while doing a presentation
- ☐ Keep hands in the right position for typing
- ☐ Don't goof off during computer class

HOMEWORK #3-3—hard copy

Classroom map

HOMEWORK	GRADE
Spend about 45 minutes on this project. When you're done, turn in the hard copy to my in box on my desk.	Submitted: 5 pts Late: -1 Protocol error: -1 Missed 0 pts

Draw a map of the computer lab. You can use KidPix, Paint, or even a blank sheet of paper. Add the two doors at either side so you can orient the rest of your drawing. Add the following items:

1. Put a red 'X' where you sit in class
2. Put a blue 'X' on traits of a good learner (My Attitudes, My Profile)
3. Put a pink 'X' where homework is posted.
4. Put a green 'X' by Lab Rules
5. Put a yellow 'X' by the printer
6. Put a black 'X' by Google Earth Map
7. Put an orange 'X' where you can see the skills you will learn this year.

HOMEWORK #3-4

HOMEWORK	GRADE
☐ Don't spend more than 45 minutes on this. ☐ Go to the class wiki (i.e., What We Did This Week) ☐ Take a print screen (prt scr); paste it into the body of email and send to me ☐ That's it!	Submitted: 5 pts Late: -1 Protocol error: -1 Missed: 0 pts

HOMEWORK #3-5—via email

Place this printout next to your keyboard. Type the lines, keeping your eyes on the text. Practice hitting the RETURN key without looking. DON'T CORRECT MISTAKES! You are trying to learn the keys NOT how to fix mistakes. This will increase your speed and your accuracy. Stop after 45 minutes. **If you are practicing at home regularly you should be seeing a big difference in your typing speed and accuracy.** Paste into body of email and send to me.

1. a;sldkfj a;sldkfj a;sldkfj a;sldkfj a;sldkfj
2. aa ;; ss ll dd kk ff jj a;sldkfj fjdksla;
3. asdf jkl; asdf jkl; fdsa ;lkj fdsa ;lkj
4. aa ;; ss ll dd kk ff jj aa ff jj dd kk ss ll aa ;;

5. aj sk dl f; aj sk dl f; ;f ld ks ja fj dk sl a;
6. la ls ld lf ka ks kd kf ja js jd jf ;a ;s ;d ;f
7. aj ak al a; sj sk sl s; dj dk dl d; fj fk fl f;
8. asd fjk ;lk fds sdf kl; lkj dsa sdf kl; fds lkj

9. as as ask ask asks asks ad ad ads ads as ask ads
10. sad sad dad dad fad fad lad lad all fall dads fads
11. all lad ask fad lass ad dad all fall ads
12. salad salsa alfalfa salad salsa alfalfa

13. as a lad; ask a dad; all fall; a sad lad; a fall; a flas; all fall; all dads; ask dad;
15. a fall ad; a sad lass; as a dad; sad dad; aa ;; ss ll dd kk ff jj a;sldkfj a;sldkfj

HOMEWORK #3-6—via email

Stop after 45 minutes

Filename protocol:
Lastname3HW#

Submitted:	*5 pts*
Late:	*-1*
Protocol error:	*-1*
Not submitted:	*0 pts*

Place this printout next to your keyboard. Type the lines, keeping your eyes on the text. Practice hitting the RETURN key without looking. DON'T CORRECT MISTAKES! You are trying to learn the keys NOT how to fix mistakes. This will increase your speed and your accuracy. Stop after 45 minutes. **If you are practicing at home regularly you should be seeing a big difference in your typing speed and accuracy.** Paste into body of email and send to me.

lol lol lol lol lol lol lol lol lol lol lol lol
lot log load hold done too to go do so of on old
gone tooth jolts fool good song sold fold told gold

frf frf frf frf frf frf frf frf frf frf frf frf frf
red rag ran far her rat tar the free jar dart dirt fir
first rake hard rail free are hare hair her red dear

aLa aLa aLa aLa aJa aJa aKa aKa aLa aLa
aHa aHa aIa aIa aOa aOa aNa aNa aNa aHa
He His Ned Nan Jan Nate Jake Is Lee Ned I Ira

note nose none done fore sore tore soar dare lone
tone gone roan thorn goat one rote fir far tar jar
for her; for those; for this; for their; for him; for the

He asked Jan to send the letter to Kari;
Here are the things that she sent to Nan;

is it to the go for he she that is the or and this these
He is; Hal sat; Nan gets; Is it; Jake is; Go to the;

HOMEWORK #3-7—via email

Place this printout next to your keyboard. Type the lines, keeping your eyes on the

HOMEWORK	GRADE
Stop after 45 minutes	Submitted: 5 pts
	Late: -1
Filename protocol:	Protocol error: -1
Lastname3HW#	Not submitted: 0 pts

text. Practice hitting the RETURN key without looking. DON'T CORRECT MISTAKES! You are trying to learn the keys NOT how to fix mistakes. This will increase your speed and your accuracy. Stop after 45 minutes. **If you are practicing at home regularly you should be seeing a big difference in your typing speed and accuracy.** Paste into body of email and send to me.

```
;p; ;p; ;p; ;p; ;p; ;p; ;p; ;p;
up; pop pat pen pet pot lap pal
k,k k,k k,k k,k k,k k,k k,k k,k
kit, kid, kin, ink, rink, ring,
;A; ;A; ;A; ;S; ;D; ;F; ;W; ;E; ;R;

pep pen pet part pug pin pan pup
go, to, the, up, lap, sit, in, see,
Find Take Dear Send All We Eat Run

When the, As there, And the, For all we,
With this, Then the, There are, The past
sip sap lap lip slop plop flop flip slip

life, like, hike, sit, hit, pit, sip,
That is, He will, I do, She did, It eats,
To Ron, Ed, Sal, Fred, Don, Dan, Sal, Dean,
```

HOMEWORK #3-8—via email

HOMEWORK	GRADE
Stop after 45 minutes	Submitted: 5 pts
	Late: -1
Filename protocol:	Protocol error: -1
Lastname3HW#	Not submitted: 0 pts

Place this printout next to your keyboard. Type the lines, keeping your eyes on the text. Practice hitting the RETURN key without looking. DON'T CORRECT MISTAKES! You are trying to learn the keys NOT how to fix mistakes. This will increase your speed and your accuracy. Stop after 45 minutes. **If you are practicing at home regularly you should be seeing a big difference in your typing speed and accuracy.** Paste into body of email and send to me.

juj juj juj juj juj juj juj juj juj juj juj juj juj
sws sws sws sws sws sws sws sws sws
jug run dug hug rug jut just our use sun fun
sew saw sow wet were wig win was won we

few sat was wag were fte drag wade dare date
junk use us fuss our four down town work two
had his use two who whose new now when was
week while with won will wall would want well
few sat was wag wig were wade rude waste wet

we are; we will; we want; we think that; the of to and in for we that is this our
of the; in the; to the; for the; on the; it is; with the; of our; and the; it is;
all an are at do for has he his if in it

we should; we would; we think; we shall; Jane John Joe Jennifer June Jan Jewell
Jill Josh

Let her go. I will too. Ned wants one also. I had a ft. of wire and an in. of twine.
I sang. Josh jogged. Helen did the work. Nan went to Ohio U. J. L. was in the jet.
Kathy went to the store. L. ft. in. Ill. Ind. Oreg. La. No. Jr.

HOMEWORK #3-9—via email

HOMEWORK	GRADE	
Stop after 45 minutes	*Submitted:*	*5 pts*
	Late:	*-1*
Filename protocol:	*Protocol error:*	*-1*
Lastname3HW#	*Not submitted:*	*0 pts*

Place this printout next to your keyboard. Type the lines, keeping your eyes on the text. Practice hitting the RETURN key without looking. DON'T CORRECT MISTAKES! You are trying to learn the keys NOT how to fix mistakes. This will increase your speed and your accuracy. Stop after 45 minutes. **If you are practicing at home regularly you should be seeing a big difference in your typing speed and accuracy.** Paste into body of email and send to me.

1. see lee fee dee led fed dead feed sea seas
2. had has he she dash lash hall heed hal
3. tea set let jet fat sat tell tall talk eat
4. feel keel leaf jell seal seek leased fed

5. hash heal shell sheds sashes ashes heals
6. jets least let fat east feat teak sat eat
7. task these dash steel leads teeth feet eat
8. lakes the these fee seals jest seek feats

9. seek the deal; at least ask a dad; a fast jet;
10. dad had the jet; he has a deal; the sale;
11. the last jet; see the last lad; the fast seal;
12. the teeth; these lads; a deal; these salads;

HOMEWORK #3-10—via email

HOMEWORK	GRADE
Stop after 45 minutes	Submitted: 5 pts
	Late: -1
Filename protocol:	Protocol error: -1
Lastname3HW#	Not submitted: 0 pts

Place this printout next to your keyboard. Type the lines, keeping your eyes on the text. Practice hitting the RETURN key without looking. DON'T CORRECT MISTAKES! You are trying to learn the keys NOT how to fix mistakes. This will increase your speed and your accuracy. Stop after 45 minutes. **If you are practicing at home regularly you should be seeing a big difference in your typing speed and accuracy.** Paste into body of email and send to me.

kit sit fit fist kid it lit hid hill fill sill
jag hag lag leg glad gas gag sag egg leg keg
nat nan den fan land hand sand fan tan than hen

tin sing kind king hint shine gain tag link
the then these this that thin than think
night sight light fight height night light
gang fang hang sang gang fang hang sang

a tall tale; a keen knight; a fine sight
he felt he needed the things at the sale
the lads asked the king at the east gate
he is a fine dad; she said he needs his kind
he had a kite; sing a little; he has a fish;

fail sail jail laid hail tail nail fail
sealing dealing keeling kneeling healing
if it is in the its a in at is it the then
is the; in the; if the; let the; see the;
fin din sin gin kin sit lit kit hit fit

HOMEWORK #3-11—via email

HOMEWORK	GRADE	
Stop after 45 minutes	Submitted:	*5 pts*
	Late:	*-1*
Filename protocol:	Protocol error:	*-1*
Lastname3HW#	Not submitted:	*0 pts*

Place this printout next to your keyboard. Type the lines, keeping your eyes on the text. Practice hitting the RETURN key without looking. DON'T CORRECT MISTAKES! You are trying to learn the keys NOT how to fix mistakes. This will increase your speed and your accuracy. Stop after 45 minutes. **If you are practicing at home regularly you should be seeing a big difference in your typing speed and accuracy.** Paste into body of email and send to me.

mom mud mam jam more time mow mad met mat
bib bit bid rib bad book bob rob sob bow
cod cup cut cow can cat tack call cot cell

most meet team same mail man comb con car
cab cob crib clam much cost cast computer
beat beam bell ball bowl bad brim better

be bet cram crab cab mince crime can munch
Right now is the time to finish the job.
One of the men will be able to sing now.
Bob brought the cat and the dog to school.
She did not like to eat hamburgers with cheese.
He did bring his lunch to the game.
Where is the crab soup that he cooked?
Oscar would like his teacher to grade his test.

HOMEWORK #3-12—via email

HOMEWORK	GRADE
Type the exercise and email it to me. Use "touch typing"—don't look at your fingers as you type!	Submitted: 5 pts Late: -1 Protocol error: -1 Not submitted: 0 pts
Stop after 45 minutes	

Bad	Vat	Hop	Tan
Sad	Raw	Mop	Van
Bar	Saw	Pop	Cap
Car	Wax	Hum	Lap
Far	Tax	Mum	Map
Tar	Sea	Yum	Nap
Sat	Tea	Dad	Rap
Vat	Bed	Had	Tap
Raw	Fed	Mad	Zap
Saw	Red	Pad	Hat
Bat	Wed	Nag	Mat
Cat	Bee	Ham	Pat
Fat	Fee	Jam	Bay
Rat	See	Can	Day
Bug	Bet	Fan	Hayden
Rug	Get	Man	Hen
Rag	Set	Pan	Men
Wag	Vet	Ran	Pen
Sat	Wet	Pet	Ten
	Hid	Yet	Let
	Lid	Bid	Net
	Rid	Did	Pie
	Pie		

HOMEWORK #3-13—via email

HOMEWORK	GRADE
Use the Excel formula for multiplication you learned in class to create a times table for fives and sixes. Come see me if you forgot how to do it. Email the spreadsheet to me.	*Submitted:* *5 pts* *Late:* *-1* *Protocol error:* *-1* *Not submitted:* *0 pts*

Stop after 45 minutes

Follow these directions:

1. Open Excel
2. Rename 'sheet1' as 'math'
3. Put a title at the top—'Math Problems'
4. Use the Excel formulas to calculate the answer
5. Remember: in the formula bar, start with =, use * to multiply (for example, =A3*A4)
6. Follow the example below for the problems:

Times Table—Fives								
5	5	5	5	5	5	5	5	5
1	2	3	4	5	6	7	8	9
5	10	15	20	25	30	35	40	45

Times Table—Sixes								
6	6	6	6	6	6	6	6	6
1	2	3	4	5	6	7	8	9
6	12	18	24	30	36	42	48	54

HOMEWORK #3-14—hard copy

HOMEWORK	GRADE	
This is a word search. Find all the words in the word bank at the bottom of the page and circle them on the diagram. Turn this sheet into my inbox. Don't take more than 45 minutes.	Submitted:	5 pts
	Late:	-1
	Protocol error:	-1
	Not submitted:	0 pts

```
R  S  D  E  E  M  G  K  R  O  W  T  E  N  J  G  I  I  K
B  A  Q  I  U  J  K  Z  C  E  L  L  S  G  N  P  W  X  P
L  A  B  T  N  T  B  B  R  Y  I  J  N  W  K  B  W  V  Y
K  R  C  L  Z  D  N  Y  J  P  G  I  O  W  M  O  U  G  P
O  S  I  K  O  W  E  E  R  T  P  D  U  Z  V  X  K  C  C
E  D  O  G  Q  O  T  N  L  Y  L  L  O  C  O  T  O  R  P
A  V  N  A  H  U  T  K  T  L  H  P  B  X  W  L  R  K  Z
S  V  Z  A  Q  T  P  H  I  N  J  I  P  H  C  K  T  R  O
U  Y  J  V  F  Q  C  R  H  F  E  R  B  X  D  Y  R  A  P
O  R  N  L  I  U  D  C  H  M  I  T  N  X  P  K  A  M  O
C  A  O  O  O  N  L  F  L  L  U  G  I  T  J  R  P  R  T
U  B  L  T  N  U  O  A  H  I  E  L  N  Q  Z  V  I  E  K
A  U  U  W  G  Y  D  C  T  J  C  E  T  P  U  H  L  T  S
J  N  B  E  S  D  M  Y  I  I  M  K  J  I  Y  E  C  A  E
T  E  Y  J  K  L  K  S  K  N  G  H  G  H  M  J  T  W  D
J  M  K  B  Q  W  X  U  G  W  L  I  F  D  D  E  Q  T  L
W  J  F  X  I  D  J  I  S  X  T  T  D  X  C  D  D  X  E
F  O  R  M  A  T  L  X  D  H  A  N  D  L  E  S  M  I  L
F  V  Y  E  V  A  G  G  Q  I  L  I  K  R  P  M  W  X  A
```

Word Bank

Alignment, GIF, PC, back-up, handles, protocol, cells, icon, right-click, clip art, indent, synonyms, desktop, menu bar, toolbar, digital, multimedia, touch, typing, drill down, netiquette, watermark, format, network

HOMEWORK #3-15—hard copy

HOMEWORK	GRADE
Complete the following crossword puzzle. Use the word bank to help. Submit to me as a hard copy (or scan into your computer and email it to me).	Submitted: 5 pts Late: -1 Protocol error: -1 Not submitted: 0 pts

Word bank:

Digital Multimedia Right-click Back-up PC Icon Desktop Toolbar Menu bar Protocol Netiquette Alignment Format Synonyms Clip art Cells Indent Watermark Drill down Network Touch typing GIF handles

ACROSS

3 A washed-out picture behind text
5 Tiny picture that activates a program
8 Graphics, pictures
9 Where a row and a column intersect in Excel
10 Adding color, borders, fonts, etc. to decorate a page
12 Electronic technology
14 Many forms of communication--audio, video, etc
15 Up/save a copy of a file to a flash drive, etc.
16 Words with similar meanings
19 What shows on your monitor before you open programs
21 The accepted way of doing things
22 Manners on the internet
23 Click/to use the mouse to bring up a drop-down menu

DOWN

1 To go through file folders to location on network
2 A collection of icons that do something
4 How text or graphics are lined up on a page
6 An animated picture, a very short movie
7 Windows-based computer
11 To type without looking at the keyboard
13 Dots around a picture that allow you to resize
17 The interconnected computers at the school
18 Words that when clicked, drop down menu of choices
20 Use the tab key to push a line in several spaces

HOMEWORK #3-16—via email

HOMEWORK	GRADE
	Submitted: 5 pts
	Late: -1
	Protocol error: -1
	Not submitted: 0 pts

Type a letter to me telling me what I should tell next year's third graders about technology class in third grade and email it to me. Include:
- What do you like about computers
- What did you find difficult
- What is your favorite computer activity
- What is your least favorite computer activity
- What advice would you give incoming third graders to help them thrive in computer class

HOMEWORK #3-17—via email

Have your parents type a letter telling me what I should advise next year's third grade parents about technology class. Include:
- Tips and secrets
- Things they found out too late
- Things that should be explained earlier and aren't
- Things that are especially valuable
- What advice they would give incoming third grade parents to help them survive computer class

The ISTE
National Educational Technology Standards and Performance Indicators for Students

1. **Creativity and Innovation**

   Students demonstrate creative thinking, construct knowledge, and develop innovative products and processes using technology. Students:
   a. apply existing knowledge to generate new ideas, products, or processes.
   b. create original works as a means of personal or group expression.
   c. use models and simulations to explore complex systems and issues.
   d. identify trends and forecast possibilities.

2. **Communication and Collaboration**

   Students use digital media and environments to communicate and work collaboratively, including at a distance, to support individual learning and contribute to the learning of others. Students:
   a. interact, collaborate, and publish with peers, experts, or others employing a variety of digital environments and media.
   b. communicate information and ideas effectively to multiple audiences using a variety of media and formats.
   c. develop cultural understanding and global awareness by engaging with learners of other cultures.
   d. contribute to project teams to produce original works or solve problems.

3. **Research and Information Fluency**

   Students apply digital tools to gather, evaluate, and use information. Students:
   a. plan strategies to guide inquiry.
   b. locate, organize, analyze, evaluate, synthesize, and ethically use information from a variety of sources and media.
   c. evaluate and select information sources and digital tools based on the appropriateness to specific tasks.
   d. process data and report results.

4. **Critical Thinking, Problem Solving, and Decision Making**

   Students use critical thinking skills to plan and conduct research, manage projects, solve problems, and make informed decisions using appropriate digital tools and resources. Students:
   a. identify and define authentic problems and significant questions for investigation.
   b. plan and manage activities to develop a solution or complete a project.
   c. collect and analyze data to identify solutions and/or make informed decisions.
   d. use multiple processes and diverse perspectives to explore alternative solutions.

5. **Digital Citizenship**

   Students understand human, cultural, and societal issues related to technology and practice legal and ethical behavior. Students:
   a. advocate and practice safe, legal, and responsible use of information and technology.
   b. exhibit a positive attitude toward using technology that supports collaboration, learning, and productivity.
   c. demonstrate personal responsibility for lifelong learning.
   d. exhibit leadership for digital citizenship.

6. **Technology Operations and Concepts**

   Students demonstrate a sound understanding of technology concepts, systems, and operations:
   a. understand and use technology systems.
   b. select and use applications effectively and productively.
   c. troubleshoot systems and applications.
   d. transfer current knowledge to learning of new technologies.

Internet Websites

1. Avatar Creator
2. Avatar creator—animal parts
3. Chess
4. Computer lab favorites
5. Edutainment games and stories
6. Edutainment
7. Geography game—geospy
8. Geography—Geonet game
9. Google Earth—free download site
10. Graphics—animated GIFs I
11. Graphics—animated GIFs II
12. Graphics—animated GIFs III
13. History—videos of events
14. How stuff works
15. Human body—body parts matching
16. Human body—the brain
17. Keyboard practice—dance mat typing
18. Keyboarding—typing test
19. Logic games
20. Mars
21. Math attack—a standard favorite
22. Math—build a bug game
23. Math/LA Videos by grade level
24. Math—Wild on Math—simple to use
25. Math—quick math
26. Music games
27. National Gallery of Art—for kids
28. Spelling—-games to learn class words
29. Stories for all ages I
30. Stories for all ages II
31. Web-based Mad Libs

Specific to Units

Animals

1. Animals
2. Animal games
3. Classify animals

Art

1. Art—Make a monster
2. Drawminos
3. Metropolitan Museum of Art
4. Minneapolis Institute of Arts
5. Mr. Picassa Head
6. Museum of Modern Art
7. National Gallery of Art—for kids

Cultures

1. African tribes
2. Egyptians
3. World National Anthems
4. Pygmies
5. Vikings

Health

1. Blood Flow
2. Body Systems

3. Build a Skeleton
4. Enchanted Learning—the body
5. Find My Body Parts
6. How the Body Works
7. Human Anatomy Online
8. Human Body
9. Human body game
10. Human Body Games
11. Human Body websites
12. Human Body—video by 2nd grade class
13. Human body—the brain
14. Human Body—videos on body parts
15. The Human Body: Respiratory System
16. Kid's Biology
17. Kid's Library page
18. Kids Konnect
19. Lots of Human Body sites to play
20. Matching Senses
21. More Human Body sites
22. Virtual Body
23. Virtual surgery
24. Weird stuff your body does
25. World Book Online

History

1. America's Story
2. America—Colonies
3. Biographies
4. Colonial America—games, etc.
5. Colonial America—life
6. Egyptian Madlibs
7. History Home on the Internet
8. History Video Guide
9. Native American Conflicts
10. Oregon Trail—virtual tour
11. USA Games
12. White House

Holidays
Groundhog Day

Keyboarding Practice

1. Alphabet rain game
2. Barracuda game
3. Bubbles game
4. Finger jig practice game
5. Free typing tutor
6. Keyboard challenge—grade level
7. Keyboard practice—quick start
8. Keyboard test—quick, adjustable
9. Keyboard—free online typing course
10. Keyboarding Fingerjig—6 minute test
11. Keyboarding for Kids
12. Keyboarding practice
13. Keyboarding resources listed
14. Keyboarding—alphabet rain game
15. Keyboarding—barracuda game
16. Keyboarding—bubbles game
17. Keyboarding—Dance Mat Typing
18. Keyboarding—full online course
19. Keyboarding—games
20. Keyboarding—lessons
21. Keyboarding—lessons and speed quiz
22. Keyboarding—more lessons
23. Keyboarding—must sign up, but free
24. Keyboarding—quick start
25. Keyboarding—speed quiz
26. Keyboard—practice with a game
27. Krazy keyboarding for kids
28. Online practice
29. Online practice—quick start
30. Online typing course
31. Online typing lessons
32. Online typing lessons — even more
33. Online typing lessons — more
34. Typing program—a graduated course

Landforms/Geography

1. About Rivers
2. Deserts
3. Explore the Colorado
4. Extreme Organisms on Earth
5. Geography Games
6. Geography Quiz Game
7. Geography Reading Problems
8. Google Earth—free download site
9. GeoNet Game
10. Labeling Maps
11. Landforms make a greeting
12. Landforms
13. Landforms—matching games, etc.
14. Learn the states
15. Los Angeles River Tour
16. Map skills
17. Mapping Game
18. Ocean animations
19. Rivers Seen from Space
20. The Colorado River
21. Virtual tour—undersea
22. What's on a Map
23. Zambezi River Tour

Language Arts

1. BiteSize—Reading, Writing, Grammar
2. Create a picture with words
3. Funny Poetry
4. Glossary of Poetry Terms
5. Grammaropolis
6. Instant Poetry—fill in the blanks
7. Poetry with a Porpoise
8. Poetry Engine
9. Shaped Poems—fun
10. Third Grade Poems
11. Parts of speech poetry
12. Web-based Mad Libs

Math

1. A Plus Math
2. Build a bug math game
3. Flashcards only
4. Flashcards or Worksheets
5. Interactive Math for Grades 2-6
6. Learn Multiplication facts—the fun way
7. Math Basics
8. Math—by Grade Level—lots of stuff
9. Math Concepts—and more
10. Math edutainment
11. Math—Grids
12. Math Grids II
13. Math Playground
14. Math practice—requires subscription
15. Math Practice Test
16. Math—Wild on Math—simple to use
17. Mental Math Drills
18. Minute Math
19. Minute math drills II
20. Number Nut Math Games
21. Pick a math category, take a quiz
22. Quick Math
23. Quick Math II
24. Speed Math
25. Test Your Math
26. Timed math
27. Timed Tests
28. Times tables
29. Virtual Manipulatives and Tessellations

Music

1. Beat Lab
2. Music Games

3. New York Philharmonic Kidzone
4. Dallas Symphony Orchestra for Kid
5. San Francisco Symphony Kids Site
6. Jake the Philharmonic Dog
7. Carnegie Hall

8. Music with hands
9. Nashville Symphony
10. Play Music
11. Classics for Kids
12. Classical KUSC

Research

1. Dictionary.com
2. Edutainment site—requires subscription
3. General info research
4. Great Research sites
5. Internet research sites for kids
6. Kids search engine for the internet
7. libraryspot.com
8. Math, reading, arcade edutainment
9. National Geographic for kids
10. Nova video programs
11. Research for kids
12. World Almanac for Kids
13. School Tube—Organized by topics
14. Science headlines—audio
15. Thesaurus.com
16. Virtual Library
17. World Book Online

Science

1. Amazing 3D world—via skateboard
2. Breathing earth—the environment
3. Cool Science for Curious Kids
4. Electric Circuits Game
5. Geo Games
6. Geography game
7. Geologic history
8. Geologic movies—great and fun
9. Mars
10. Plant life cycle
11. **Redwood Forests video**
12. Science games
13. Science Games II
14. Science Games—Bitesize
15. Science interactive—plates, etc
16. Science stories—audio and textual
17. Science stories—video
18. Science Stuff
19. Solar System Video
20. Solar System in 3D
21. Stardate Online
22. Virtual tour (with pictures) of a zoo
23. Virtual tours
24. Virtual weather, machines and surgery
25. Water Cycle—animated

Spanish

1. Spanish resources

2. Spanish Stories

Stories

1. Get Writing—write your own story
2. Make another story
3. Make yet another story
4. Make your story a newspaper clipping
5. Mighty Book
6. Stories to read for youngsters
7. Stories to read from PBS kids
8. Stories to read from PBS kids
9. Stories to read—II
10. Stories to read

11. Stories to read—International Library
12. Storybook Maker
13. Web version of Mad Libs

Technology

1. Bad guy Patrol
2. Computer basics
3. Computer Basics II
4. Computer puzzle
5. Find the Technology
6. Faux Paws Internet Safety
7. Internet Safety
8. NASA Kids Club
9. Organize technology (drag and drop)
10. Parts of the computer
11. Videos on Computer Basics K-6
12. Who are your online friends?

USA

1. Colonial America
2. USA Puzzle
3. All About America

Water Cycle
How the water cycle works

Word Study

1. Dolch Site Word Activities
2. Grammar—Adjectives
3. Grammar games
4. High-frequency words—hangman
5. High-frequency words—practice
6. Spelling practice—use with spelling words
7. Stories with Dolch Words
8. Vocabulary Fun
9. Word Central—from Merriam Webster
10. Word Games
11. Word Videos

Miscellaneous

1. 360° views from around the world
2. Christmas site
3. Edutainment
4. Minyanland
5. More Worldwide webcams for kids
6. Quick quizzes—how much do you know?
7. Thinking Skills—Riddles
8. USA Puzzle
9. Web cams from around the world
10. Whitehouse kids' site

For teachers

1. Analyze, read, write literature
2. Animations, assessments, charts, more
3. Biomes/Habitats—for teachers
4. Children's University
5. Create a magazine cover
6. Create free activities/diagrams in a Flash!
7. Creative Tools
8. Crossword Puzzle Maker
9. Easy Techie Stuff for the Classroom
10. Easy-to-navigate collection
11. Environmental footprint
12. Geography Activities—for teachers
13. Glogster—posters
14. Google Earth Lesson Plans I

15. Google Earth Lesson Plans II
16. Google Earth in Math Curriculum
17. Hollywood Sq/Jeopardy Templates
18. How to Videos for Web 2.0
19. K-8 school-related videos. Tons of them
20. Make digital posters
21. Miscellaneous links
22. Miscellaneous links II
23. Online quizzes you create, online grades
24. Password creator
25. Posters—8x10 at a time—simple
26. PowerPoint Templates
27. Print Large Posters in 8x10 bits
28. Print Posters One Page at a Time
29. Publish the magazines
30. Pupil Tube
31. Shelfari—share books with students
32. So many Free online tools (Web 2.0)
33. Tag clouds
34. Tools for studying writing
35. Training videos
36. Turn pictures into Videos—Easily
37. Turn short stories into books
38. Vocab, prefix/suffix, word lists and more

INDEX